New Directions for
Community Colleges

Arthur M. Cohen
EDITOR-IN-CHIEF

Caroline Q. Durdella
Nathan R. Durdella
ASSOCIATE EDITORS

Amy Fara Edwards
MANAGING EDITOR

Community College Faculty Scholarship

John M. Braxton

EDITOR

Number 171 • Fall 2015
Jossey-Bass
San Francisco

COMMUNITY COLLEGE FACULTY SCHOLARSHIP
John M. Braxton (ed.)
New Directions for Community Colleges, no. 171

Arthur M. Cohen, Editor-in-Chief
Caroline Q. Durdella, Nathan R. Durdella, Associate Editors
Amy Fara Edwards, Managing Editor

NEW DIRECTIONS FOR COMMUNITY COLLEGES (ISSN 0194-3081, electronic ISSN 1536-0733) is part of The Jossey-Bass Higher and Adult Education Series and is published quarterly by Wiley Subscription Services, Inc., A Wiley Company, at Jossey-Bass, One Montgomery St., Ste. 1200, San Francisco, CA 94104. POSTMASTER: Send address changes to New Directions for Community Colleges, Jossey-Bass, One Montgomery St., Ste. 1200, San Francisco, CA 94104.

SUBSCRIPTIONS cost $89 for individuals in the U.S., Canada, and Mexico, and $113 in the rest of the world for print only; $89 in all regions for electronic only; $98 in the U.S., Canada, and Mexico for combined print and electronic; $122 for combined print and electronic in the rest of the world. Institutional print only subscriptions are $335 in the U.S., $375 in Canada and Mexico, and $409 in the rest of the world; electronic only subscriptions are $335 in all regions; combined print and electronic subscriptions are $402 in the U.S., $442 in Canada and Mexico, and $476 in the rest of the world.

Cover design: Wiley
Cover Images: © Lava 4 images | Shutterstock

EDITORIAL CORRESPONDENCE should be sent to the Editor-in-Chief, Arthur M. Cohen, at 1749 Mandeville Lane, Los Angeles, CA 90049. All manuscripts receive anonymous reviews by external referees.

New Directions for Community Colleges is indexed in CIJE: Current Index to Journals in Education (ERIC), Contents Pages in Education (T&F), Current Abstracts (EBSCO), Ed/Net (Simpson Communications), Education Index/Abstracts (H. W. Wilson), Educational Research Abstracts Online (T&F), ERIC Database (Education Resources Information Center), and Resources in Education (ERIC).

Microfilm copies of issues and articles are available in 16mm and 35mm, as well as microfiche in 105mm, through University Microfilms Inc., 300 North Zeeb Road, Ann Arbor, MI 48106-1346.

CONTENTS

EDITOR'S NOTES   1
John M. Braxton

1. Community College Faculty Engagement in Boyer's Domains   7
of Scholarship
John M. Braxton, Dawn Lyken-Segosebe
This chapter describes the findings from a national survey of community college faculty. With the lens of Boyer's Domains of Scholarship
applied to these findings, a more fine-grained and accurate assessment
of the engagement of community college faculty members in scholarship emerges.

2. Types of Faculty Scholars in Community Colleges   15
Toby J. Park, John M. Braxton, Dawn Lyken-Segosebe
This chapter describes three empirically derived types of faculty scholars in community colleges: Immersed Scholars, Scholars of Dissemination, and Scholars of Pedagogical Knowledge. This chapter discusses
these types and offers a recommendation.

3. Faculty Scholarship at Community Colleges: Culture,   21
Institutional Structures, and Socialization
Vanessa Smith Morest
This chapter looks at community college faculty engagement in scholarship. Community college faculty spend the majority of their time engaged in teaching, and therefore their scholarship typically focuses on
strengthening curriculum and instruction. The paper identifies some
of the structural and cultural challenges and supports to scholarship at
community colleges. The author concludes that mechanisms for encouraging and rewarding scholarship at community colleges remain
underutilized.

4. Scholarship and the Professional Identity of Community   37
College Faculty Members
James C. Palmer
Professional associations established by and for community college fac-
ulty have forged a path to an alternative professional identity that rec-
ognizes disciplinary scholarship as an essential part of faculty work.

5. A National Initiative of Teaching, Researching, and 49
Dreaming: Community College Faculty Research in "Achieving
the Dream" Colleges
Linda Serra Hagedorn
The Achieving the Dream initiative have created a new environment
and new forms of thinking among faculty that has spurred some to
action research within their classrooms and beyond.

6. Filling the Void: The Roles of a Local Applied Research 63
Center and a Statewide Workforce Training Consortium
Richard C. Perniciaro, Lawrence A. Nespoli, Sivaraman Anbarasan
This chapter describes the development of an applied research center at
Atlantic Cape Community College and a statewide workforce training
consortium run by the community college sector in New Jersey.

7. Tweaking the Culture of the Community College 77
John M. Braxton, William R. Doyle, Dawn Lyken-Segosebe
This chapter contends that scholarship should become a part of the
mission of the community college. The authors describe actions for individual community colleges and state and federal actions that encourage and support the engagement of community college faculty members in scholarship.

Appendix: Description of Research Methods and Analyses for 87
Chapters 1 and 2
John M. Braxton
This appendix describes the methodology and statistical procedures
used to obtain the findings presented in Chapters 1 and 2. The ap-
pendix also contains Tables A.1 to A.4.

INDEX 97

Editor's Notes

Teaching constitutes the primary role of faculty members in community colleges. Teaching occupies 85% of the typical community college faculty member's time (Rosser & Townsend, 2006). This time commitment includes such aspects of teaching as preparing for class, classroom instruction, grading student assignments, and advising students (Rosser & Townsend, 2006). Despite this extensive engagement in teaching, three factors give rise to the question: To what extent are community college faculty members engaged in research and scholarship?

The first of these factors concerns the proportion of full-time community college faculty members who hold a doctoral degree. Although the majority of community college faculty members hold a master's degree, 19% of them have received a doctoral degree (Townsend & Rosser, 2009). Given that the thrust of the doctoral socialization process centers on the acquisition of attitudes, values, knowledge, and skills for scholarly role performance (Austin & Wulff, 2004), we might expect some engagement in scholarship by doctorate-holding community college faculty members.

Another factor concerns the professional identity of community college faculty members, an identity that remains elusive (Cohen & Brawer, 2008). A host of scholars contend that involvement in scholarship provides a vehicle for the forging of the professional identity of community college faculty (Cohen & Brawer, 2003; Eaton, 1994; Levin, Kater, & Wagoner, 2006; Outcalt, 2002; Palmer, 1992; Prager, 2003; Vaughan, 1988).

An alignment of the education mission of the community college with higher education rather than secondary education through faculty engagement in scholarship constitutes the third factor (Crocker-Lakness, 1984; Seidman, 1985). Put differently, the pursuit of scholarship differentiates the mission of higher education from that of secondary education as the advancement of knowledge constitutes one of the primary missions of higher education. Advancements in knowledge find expression in the research and scholarship of faculty members.

Taken together, these three factors reinforce the significance of the question: To what extent are community college faculty members engaged in research and scholarship? This question begets other questions such as: What are the types of research and scholarship performed by community college faculty members? What are the various forces that either foster or impede the engagement of community college members in research and scholarship? Are there specific examples of community college faculty

New Directions for Community Colleges, no. 171, Fall 2015 © 2015 Wiley Periodicals, Inc.
Published online in Wiley Online Library (wileyonlinelibrary.com) • DOI: 10.1002/cc.20149

research and scholarship that demonstrate the value of such work to both the institution and to larger society? How can individual community colleges and local and state policy makers support some community college faculty in their engagement in research and scholarship?

This issue of *New Directions for Community Colleges* titled "Community College Faculty Scholarship" addresses these questions. This volume consists of seven chapters.

The first two chapters concentrate on the extent to which community college faculty members are engaged in research and scholarship as well as on the types of scholarship pursued. In Chapter 1, "Community College Faculty Engagement in Boyer's Domains of Scholarship," John M. Braxton and Dawn Lyken-Segosebe assess the extent of community college engagement in Boyer's (1990) four scholarship domains of application, discovery, integration, and teaching. They gauge the extent of engagement in these four domains using both publications and unpublished, publicly observable outcomes of scholarship as indicators of engagement. Given Boyer's (1990) call for using scholarly forms distinct from journal articles, book chapters, and books in the assessment of faculty scholarship, Braxton and Lyken-Segosebe used such unpublished, publicly observable outcomes of scholarship. Using the results of a national sample of 348 full-time community college faculty members, they describe the general level of community college faculty engagement in each of the four domains of scholarship as well as differences by the highest earned degree, academic rank, and academic discipline. In Chapter 2, Toby J. Park, John M. Braxton, and Dawn Lyken-Segosebe further depict the types of scholarship engaged in by community college faculty members. In this chapter titled "Types of Faculty Scholars in Community Colleges," these authors unpack engagement in each of the four domains of scholarship by empirically deriving three types of faculty scholars in community colleges. Park, Braxton, and Lyken-Segosebe describe these three types of faculty scholars and how they differ by race/ethnicity, academic rank, academic discipline, highest earned degree held, and tenure status.

The first two chapters indicate that community college faculty members do engage to some extent in various types of scholarship and that three types of faculty scholars exist. However, Vanessa Smith Morest points out in her chapter titled "Faculty Scholarship at Community Colleges: Culture, Institutional Structures, and Socialization" that "increasing the role of community college faculty in scholarship requires policies and structures that support and reward these efforts" (p. 22). In this third chapter, she delineates internal and external forces that foster or impede the development of institutional cultures that support the engagement of community college faculty in scholarship. Morest also offers three recommendations for ways community colleges can identify and reward their faculty for their engagement in scholarship.

Professional associations for community college faculty members in specific academic disciplines constitute a force that fosters the engagement in scholarship by community college faculty members. In Chapter 4, "Scholarship and the Professional Identity of Community College Faculty Members," James C. Palmer describes the roles of national associations that involve community college faculty members such as the American Mathematical Association of Two-Year Colleges, the Committee on Physics in Two-Year Colleges, and the Two-Year College English Association in forging a professional identity for community college faculty members that acknowledges scholarship as a part of the work of community college faculty members. Palmer offers some suggestions for professional associations, scholars who study the community college and the leadership of community colleges to further develop such a professional identity for community college faculty members.

Chapters 5 and 6 provide specific examples of community college faculty research and scholarship that demonstrate the value of their work both to the institution and to larger society. In Chapter 5, Linda Serra Hagedorn describes the role of the *Achieving the Dream: Community Colleges Count* initiative funded by the Lumina Foundation in stimulating research by community college faculty members on ways to improve their teaching and foster student success. In this chapter titled "A National Initiative of Teaching, Researching, and Dreaming: Community College Faculty Research in 'Achieving the Dream' Colleges," Hagedorn describes faculty-led research in three community colleges participating in the Achieving the Dream project. Through vignettes of faculty research in each of the three colleges, Hagedorn demonstrates the value of such research to these three colleges. This chapter also gives concrete illustrations of community college faculty engagement in Boyer's scholarship of teaching domain discussed in Chapter 1.

The value to the state and the local community of applied research in community colleges receives attention in Chapter 6, "Filling the Void: The Roles of a Local Applied Research Center and a Statewide Workforce Training Consortium" by Richard C. Perniciaro, Lawrence A. Nespoli, and Sivaraman Anbarasan. This chapter describes a consortium of community colleges in New Jersey created to develop training programs to meet the needs of businesses for skilled workers. Faculty members in community colleges in the state of New Jersey participate in this process by conducting applied research in collaboration with businesses that delineates demands of different jobs and then through curriculum development. This chapter also describes the creation of the Center for Regional and Business Research at Atlantic Cape Community College to meet the needs of businesses and other organizations in the local community. Examples of applied research conducted include enrollment projects of student enrollment to school districts in the region served by the college, economic impact studies, market research, and economic development strategies. This center provides a structure for participation in the scholarship of application (engagement) by faculty at Atlantic Cape Community College.

In Chapter 7, the last chapter of this volume, John M. Braxton, William R. Doyle, and Dawn Lyken-Segosebe present recommendations for institutional, local, and state-level policy and practices centered on supporting community college faculty engagement in scholarship. This chapter bears the title "Tweaking the Culture of the Community College."

Public policy makers, members of governing boards of community colleges, presidents, and chief academic affairs officers of community colleges constitute the primary intended audience for this volume. Moreover, scholars of the academic profession in general and of the professoriate of the community college as well as students in graduate-level courses in higher education preparation programs will also find much of value in this volume.

John M. Braxton
Editor

References

Austin, A., & Wulff, D. (2004). The challenge to prepare the next generation of faculty. In *Paths to the professoriate: Strategies for enriching the preparation of future faculty* (pp. 1–16). San Francisco, CA: Jossey-Bass.

Boyer, E. L. (1990). *Scholarship reconsidered: Priorities of the professoriate*. Princeton, NJ: Carnegie Foundation for the Advancement of Teaching.

Cohen, A. M., & Brawer, F. B. (2003). *The American community college* (4th. ed.). San Francisco, CA: Jossey-Bass.

Cohen, A. M., & Brawer, F. B. (2008). *The American community college* (5th ed.). San Francisco, CA: Jossey-Bass.

Crocker-Lakness, J. (1984). Community college faculty should engage in research for publication. *Association for Communication Administration Bulletin, 47*, 78–80. (ERIC Document Reproduction Service No. EJ 292 965)

Eaton, J. S. (1994). All access is not equal: The need for collegiate education in community colleges. In A. M. Cohen (Ed.), *New Directions for Community Colleges: No. 86. Relating curriculum and transfer* (pp. 3–11). San Francisco, CA: Jossey-Bass.

Levin, J. S., Kater, S., & Wagoner, R. L. (2006). *Community college faculty: At work in the new economy*. New York: Palgrave Macmillan.

Outcalt, C. L. (2002). Toward a professionalized community college professoriate. In C. L. Outcalt (Ed.), *New Directions for Community Colleges: No. 118. Community college faculty: Characteristics, practices, and challenges* (pp. 109–115). San Francisco, CA: Jossey-Bass.

Palmer, J. (1992). Faculty professionalism reconsidered. In K. Kroll (Ed.), *New Directions for Community Colleges: No. 79. Maintaining faculty excellence* (pp. 29–38). San Francisco, CA: Jossey-Bass.

Prager, C. (2003). Scholarship matters. *Community College Journal of Research and Practice, 27*, 579–592. doi:10.1080/10668920390194499

Rosser, V. J., & Townsend, B. K. (2006). Determining public 2-year college faculty's intent to leave: An empirical model. *The Journal of Higher Education, 77*(1), 124–147.

Seidman, E. (1985). *In the words of the faculty*. San Francisco, CA: Jossey-Bass.

Townsend, B. K., & Rosser, V. J. (2009). The extent and nature of scholarly activities among community college faculty. *Community College Journal of Research and Practice*, *33*, 669–681. doi:10.1080/10668920902921502

Vaughan, G. B. (1988). Scholarship in community colleges: The path to respect. *The Educational Record*, *69*(2), 26–31.

JOHN M. BRAXTON is a professor of education in the Higher Education Leadership and Policy Program at Peabody College of Vanderbilt University.

NEW DIRECTIONS FOR COMMUNITY COLLEGES • DOI: 10.1002/cc

1

This chapter describes the findings from a national survey of community college faculty. With the lens of Boyer's Domains of Scholarship applied to these findings, a more fine-grained and accurate assessment of the engagement of community college faculty members in scholarship emerges.

Community College Faculty Engagement in Boyer's Domains of Scholarship

John M. Braxton, Dawn Lyken-Segosebe

Teaching constitutes the primary role of faculty members in community colleges. Teaching occupies 85% of the typical community college faculty member's time (Rosser & Townsend, 2006). Moreover, research on faculty publication productivity suggests that community college faculty members publish very infrequently. More specifically, data from the 2004 National Survey of Postsecondary Faculty (NSOPF:04) indicates that community college faculty members have published an average of less than one article in both refereed and nonrefereed journals during the past 2 years (Rosser & Townsend, 2006). Moreover, nearly 70% of community college faculty reported having no publications during a 2-year period (Schuster & Finkelstein, 2006). These rates provide only a general measure of article production and may produce an inaccurate indicator of the level of community college faculty members' participation in research and scholarship. However, a different picture of the engagement in scholarship by community college faculty members might emerge through the use of the lens of Boyer's perspective on scholarship encapsulated in his 1990 volume *Scholarship Reconsidered: Priorities of the Professoriate.*

Boyer offers two perspectives that might produce a different picture of the engagement of community college faculty members in research and scholarship. One perspective centers on his call to broaden the definition of scholarship beyond the predominant emphasis on the scholarship of discovery to include the scholarships of application, integration, and teaching (Boyer, 1990).

NEW DIRECTIONS FOR COMMUNITY COLLEGES, no. 171, Fall 2015 © 2015 Wiley Periodicals, Inc.
Published online in Wiley Online Library (wileyonlinelibrary.com) • DOI: 10.1002/cc.20150

According to Boyer (1990), the scholarship of application involves the application of disciplinary knowledge and skill to help address important societal and institutional problems, whereas the acquisition of knowledge for its own sake constitutes the aim of the scholarship of discovery. The testing and generation of theory is also an essential facet of the scholarship of discovery. The scholarship of integration requires scholars who give meaning to isolated facts, illuminate data in a revealing way, make connections across the discipline, and synthesize the knowledge of the discipline. Rice (1991) clarifies that domain of scholarship by asserting "scholars are needed with a capacity to synthesize, to look for new relationships between the parts and the whole, to relate the past and future to the present, and to ferret out patterns of meaning that cannot be seen through traditional disciplinary lenses" (p. 13). The development and improvement of pedagogical practice constitutes the goal of the scholarship of teaching (Braxton, Luckey, & Helland, 2002).

Of these four domains of scholarship, Boyer (1990, pp. 60–61) viewed engagement in the scholarship of application and the scholarship of teaching as befitting community college faculty members. Thus, we might expect that community college faculty engagement may vary across these four domains of scholarship, a variation obscured by the use of a general measure of article production. Boyer also argued for flexibility in what counts as scholarship. He argued for the use of scholarly forms distinct from journal articles, book chapters, and books in the assessment of faculty scholarship (Boyer, 1990). Thus, he was arguing for the use of other forms of writing or documented evidence of scholarship. Shulman and Hutchings (1998) contend that an unpublished outcome of scholarship may be designated as scholarship if it meets three necessary characteristics: (a) it must be publicly observable, (b) it must be amenable to critical appraisal, and (c) it must be in a form that permits its exchange and use by other members of a scholarly community. By expanding the definition of what counts as scholarship to include unpublished, but publicly observable, outcomes of scholarship, a different picture of the level of community college faculty member engagement in research and scholarship may emerge.

Although research on the extent of faculty engagement in each of Boyer's four domains of scholarship has been conducted in 4-year colleges and universities (Braxton et al., 2002), little or no research has transpired on the engagement of community college faculty members in each of Boyer's four domains of scholarship. As a consequence, the findings we describe in this chapter address this lack of research by attending to the following four questions.

Question One: Does the proportion of community college faculty members having no publications during the past 3 years vary across the four domains of scholarship delineated by Boyer? As stated previously, nearly 70% of community college faculty members registered no publications during a 2-year period. This first question concentrates on whether the proportion of community college faculty members' engagement in each of the four domains of scholarship resembles this general level of publication productivity, or reference point, for community college faculty members.

Question Two: Do community college faculty members with a doctoral degree differ in their level of engagement in the four domains of scholarship from their colleagues who do not have a doctoral degree? Given the thrust of the doctoral socialization process on the acquisitions of attitudes, values, knowledge, and skills of research (Austin & Wulff, 2004), we might expect that community college faculty members holding a doctoral degree would exhibit a higher degree of engagement in each of the four domains of scholarship than their non-doctoral-degree-holding faculty counterparts.

Question Three: Do community college faculty members' levels of engagement in the four domains of scholarship vary by their academic rank? In his review of literature on the correlates of faculty publication productivity, Creswell (1985) noted a relationship between academic rank and faculty publication productivity.

Question Four: Do community college faculty members' levels of engagement in the four domains of scholarship vary across different academic disciplines? From their review of research on disciplinary differences, Braxton and Hargens (1996) concluded that the differences among academic disciplines are "profound and extensive." More specifically, the level of paradigmatic development of an academic discipline affects teaching and research activities. Moreover, Braxton, Luckey, and Helland (2002) found discipline differences in 4-year college and university faculty engagement in two of the four domains of scholarship described by Boyer (1990): the scholarship of application and the scholarship of teaching.

We describe the methods and statistical analyses we used to address these four questions in the appendix to this volume. A description of the variables used to address these questions is available from the first author. In addition, readers interested in the professional behaviors pertinent to publications and unpublished outcomes of scholarship indicative of the four domains of scholarship described by Boyer (1990) should consult "Appendix B: The Inventory of Scholarship" in Braxton, Luckey, and Helland's (2002) volume *Institutionalizing a Broader View of Scholarship Through Boyer's Four Domains.*

Findings

We organized the presentation of our findings by the four research questions.

Question One: Does the proportion of community college faculty members having no publications during the past 3 years vary across the four domains of scholarship delineated by Boyer? In attending to this question, we used the previously delineated reference point of 70% of community college faculty members registering no publications during a 2-year period. This reference point refers to a general, undifferentiated measure of 2-year publication productivity. Table A.1 in the appendix displays these various percentages presented in response to this first research question.

We learned that the percentage of community college faculty members who report no publications during the past 3 years exceeds this point of reference for publications reflecting the scholarship of application (87.4%), discovery (80.6%), and teaching (86.2%). Examples of publications reflective of the scholarship of application include a refereed journal article reporting findings of research designed to solve a practical problem and an article that applies new disciplinary knowledge to a practical problem. A refereed journal article reporting findings of research designed to gain new knowledge constitutes an example of a discovery-oriented publication. Examples of publications directed toward the scholarship of teaching include the use of a new instructional method and reporting a new teaching approach developed by the individual faculty member.

However, the percentage of community college faculty members registering no publications associated with the scholarship of integration falls considerably below this reference point given that 55.3% of community college faculty members report having no publications reflective of this domain of scholarship. Moreover, more than two fifths (43.7%) of community college faculty members have published one to two times within this domain. Examples of publications associated with the scholarship of integration embrace a review of literature on a disciplinary topic and a review essay of two or more books on similar topics.

We obtain a different picture of the level of engagement in research and scholarship by full-time community college faculty members when we consider the proportion of such faculty members who report no unpublished outcomes of scholarship reflective of the scholarships of application (24.8%), integration (38.8%), and teaching (0.6%). Put another way, the majority of community college faculty members report they have produced one to two times unpublished outcomes of scholarship associated with the domains of application (70.7%) and of integration (57.1%). Moreover, more than half (51.3%) of community college faculty members report that they have produced three to five times forms of unpublished outcomes of scholarship associated with the scholarship of teaching. Conducting a study for a local governmental organization and conducting a study to help solve a community problem provide examples of unpublished outcomes of scholarship reflective of the scholarships of application. Giving a public lecture on a current topic in your discipline to a local high school class and giving a public talk on a current topic in your discipline on a local radio station offer examples of unpublished outcomes of scholarship associated

NEW DIRECTIONS FOR COMMUNITY COLLEGES • DOI: 10.1002/cc

with the scholarship of integration. Examples of unpublished outcomes of scholarship associated with the scholarship of teaching consist of making a presentation to colleagues about new instructional techniques and developing examples, materials, class exercises, or assignments that help students to learn difficult course concepts.

Question Two: Do community college faculty members with a doctoral degree differ in their level of engagement in the four domains of scholarship from their colleagues who do not have a doctoral degree? As we previously posited the thrust of the doctoral socialization process centers on the acquisition of attitudes, values, knowledge, and skills of research (Austin & Wulff, 2004). Accordingly, we might expect that community college faculty members holding a doctoral degree would exhibit a higher degree of engagement in each of the four domains of scholarship than their non-doctoral-degree-holding faculty counterparts. However, we learned those community college faculty holding a doctoral degree differ little from their non-doctoral-degree-holding faculty colleagues on their level of engagement in each of the seven dependent variables. A table reporting the results of the statistical tests made to address this question is available upon request from the first author.

Question Three: Do community college faculty members' levels of engagement in the four domains of scholarship vary by their academic rank? The answer to this question is no, as we found that the academic rank of community college faculty members makes little or no difference in their level of engagement across the four domains of scholarship using both publications and unpublished, but publicly observable, outcomes as indices of engagement. A table displaying the results of the statistical tests made to address this question is available from the first author.

Question Four: Do community college faculty members' levels of engagement in the four domains of scholarship vary across different academic disciplines? We learned the academic discipline of the community college faculty member makes little or no difference in their level of performance of publications reflective of the scholarship of discovery and the scholarship of teaching. However, academic discipline does matter in level of publications oriented toward the scholarship of application and the scholarship of integration. More specifically, community college faculty members who are historians and sociologists tend to exhibit higher levels of publications reflective of the scholarship of application than do their colleagues in biology. Academic sociologists in community colleges also tend to produce a higher level of publications oriented toward the scholarship of integration than do their colleagues in chemistry. Moreover, academic historians and sociologists in community colleges also tend to enact more unpublished outcomes directed toward the scholarship of integration than their counterparts in biology and chemistry. Table A.2 of the appendix provides the supporting results of the statistical analyses conducted.

Conclusions and Implications for Practice

We present the following two conclusions that we derive from the configuration of findings of this study. First, the two perspectives on scholarship advanced by Boyer (1990) provide a more fine-grained and accurate assessment of the engagement of community college faculty members in scholarship. Our findings indicate that the use of a general measure of article publication productivity provides an inaccurate picture of the publication productivity of community college faculty members. Although the percentage of community college faculty members who report no publications associated with the scholarships of application, discovery, and teaching during the past 3 years exceeds the previously described reference point of 70%, the percentage of community college faculty members registering no publications associated with the scholarship of integration falls considerably below this point of reference. Moreover, more than two fifths of community college faculty members have published one to two times within this domain within the past 3 years. Thus, community college faculty members exhibit a level of engagement in the scholarship of integration that would go unidentified without the application of the lens of Boyer's four domains of scholarship to assess research and scholarship performance.

Our findings also indicate that the use of publications as the indicator of research and scholarship underestimates the level of full-time community college faculty members' level of engagement in scholarship of application and teaching. As previously indicated, Boyer (1990) argued for use of other forms of writing or documented evidence of scholarship distinct from journal articles, book chapters, and books to assess faculty scholarship (Boyer, 1990). With the use of unpublished outcomes of scholarship as an indicator of their engagement, we conclude that full-time community college faculty members exhibit greater levels of engagement in the scholarship of application and teaching than suggested by the use of publications within these domains. Thus, we conclude that publications within the four domains of scholarship and unpublished outcomes of scholarship associated with Boyer's domains as used in this study provide a more complete and accurate picture of the level of engagement in scholarship by full-time community college faculty members.

The second conclusion takes the following form. As previously discussed, many scholars view the professional identity of community college faculty members as uncertain. Scholars such as Palmer (1992) and Vaughan (1988) view scholarship as a basis for the forging of a professional identity for community college faculty members. We conclude that the pursuit of application-, integration-, and teaching-oriented scholarship offers a starting point for development of the professional identity of full-time community college faculty members. For faculty in history and sociology, the shaping of an identity grounded in the scholarship of application and integration looms more likely than for faculty in biology and chemistry. An identity rooted in the scholarship of teaching seems particularly promising given that the scholarship of teaching seeks to develop and refine pedagogical practice (Braxton et al., 2002). As such, the scholarship of teaching resonates with the scholastic and the classroom research frames of Palmer's (1992) frames of reference for the professional identity of community college faculty members.

From these two conclusions, we offer three implications for practice. First, future measurements of the engagement of full-time community college faculty members in scholarship should use the two types of indicators used in this study: publications reflecting each of the four domains of scholarship delineated by Boyer and unpublished, publicly observable outcomes of scholarship reflective of Boyer's domains. To do so provides a fuller picture of the engagement in scholarship by full-time community college faculty members.

Second, we boldly suggest that community colleges should begin discussions about including the pursuit of the scholarship of application, integration, and teaching by full-time faculty members into their institutional missions. Acknowledgment of scholarship as part of the mission of the community college would accelerate the development of the professional identity of full-time community college faculty members, an identity ingrained in the pursuit of the scholarships of application, integration, and teaching. Such an inclusion, however, should not come at the expense of teaching as the core mission of the community college. Moreover, such an addition would also not place faculty at a disadvantage because of their highest earned degree or their academic rank given our findings regarding research questions two and three.

Third, the academic reward structure—reappointments, tenure, promotion, and annual salary adjustments—of those community colleges that include scholarship in their institutional missions need to give some weight to those faculty members who elect to engage in scholarship associated with the domains of application, integration, and teaching. The specific forms of scholarship displayed in Table A.1 provide a foundation for such assessments. In particular, we stress the importance of encouraging faculty to submit for review their unpublished outcomes of scholarship that meet Shulman and Hutchings's (1998) three necessary characteristics for designating an outcome as scholarship, which we previously described. Accordingly, their work should be in the form of audio- and videotaped presentations, papers, reports, and websites so as to meet these three criteria (Braxton & Del Favero, 2002).

Closing Thought

In their important volume *Community College Faculty: Overlooked and Undervalued*, Townsend and Twombly (2007) contend that "scholars and community college administrators should focus attention on sharpening the role of community college faculty members around which their professional identity is built and then on how new faculty members are socialized to this professional identity" (p. 117). We assert that the implementation of the three implications for practice would contribute to the sharpening of the professional identity of community college faculty members, an identity that includes engagement in scholarship.

References

Austin, A., & Wulff, D. (2004). The challenge to prepare the next generation of faculty. In *Paths to the professoriate: Strategies for enriching the preparation of future faculty* (pp. 1–16). San Francisco, CA: Jossey-Bass.

Boyer, E. L. (1990). *Scholarship reconsidered: Priorities of the professoriate*. Princeton, NJ: Carnegie Foundation for the Advancement of Teaching.

Braxton, J. M., & Del Favero, M. (2002). Evaluating scholarship performance: Traditional and emergent assessment templates. In C. L. Colbeck (Ed.), *New Directions for Institutional Research: No. 114. Evaluating faculty performance* (pp. 19–32). San Francisco, CA: Jossey-Bass.

Braxton, J. M., & Hargens, L. (1996). Variation among academic disciplines: Analytical frameworks and research. In J. Smart (Ed.), *Higher education: Handbook of research and theory* (Vol. 11, pp. 1–46). New York, NY: Agathun Press.

Braxton, J. M., Luckey, W., & Helland, P. (2002). *Institutionalizing a broader view of scholarship through Boyer's four domains* (ASHE-ERIC Higher Education Report, Volume 29, Number 2). San Francisco, CA: Jossey-Bass.

Creswell, J. W. (1985). *Faculty research performance: Lessons from the sciences and social sciences* (ASHE-ERIC Higher Education Report, Volume 14, Number 4). Washington, DC: Association for the Study of Higher Education.

Palmer, J. (1992). Faculty professionalism reconsidered. In K. Kroll (Ed.), *New Directions for Community Colleges: No. 79. Maintaining faculty excellence* (pp. 29–38). San Francisco, CA: Jossey-Bass.

Rice, E. (1991). The new American scholar: Scholarship and the purposes of the university. *Metropolitan Universities, 1*, 7–18.

Rosser, V. J., & Townsend, B. K. (2006). Determining public 2-year college faculty's intent to leave: An empirical model. *The Journal of Higher Education, 77*(1), 124–147.

Schuster, J. H., & Finkelstein, M. J. (2006). *The American faculty: The restructuring of academic work and careers*. Baltimore, MD: Johns Hopkins University Press.

Shulman, L. S., & Hutchings, P. (1998). *About the scholarship of teaching and learning: The Pew scholars national fellowship program*. Menlo Park, CA: The Carnegie Foundation for the Advancement of Teaching.

Townsend, B. K., & Twombly, S. B. (2007). *Community college faculty: Overlooked and undervalued* (ASHE Higher Education Report, Volume 32, Number 6). San Francisco, CA: Jossey-Bass.

Vaughan, G. B. (1988). Scholarship in community colleges: The path to respect. *The Educational Record, 69*(2), 26–31.

JOHN M. BRAXTON *is a professor of education in the Higher Education Leadership and Policy Program at Peabody College of Vanderbilt University.*

DAWN LYKEN-SEGOSEBE *received her PhD in leadership and policy studies from Vanderbilt University.*

2

This chapter describes three empirically derived types of faculty scholars in community colleges: Immersed Scholars, Scholars of Dissemination, and Scholars of Pedagogical Knowledge. This chapter discusses these types and offers a recommendation.

Types of Faculty Scholars in Community Colleges

Toby J. Park, John M. Braxton, Dawn Lyken-Segosebe

The definition of scholarship was forever changed when Boyer (1990) suggested that it be expanded beyond the traditional scholarship of discovery to also include the scholarship of integration, the scholarship of application, and the scholarship of teaching. Although Boyer's text has given rise to a number of studies focusing on the meaning of the domains of scholarship (e.g., Glassick, Huber, & Maeroff, 1997; Shulman & Hutchings, 1998), additional research has also focused on the interplay between the four domains and their composition of an overall social system of scholarship (e.g., Braxton, Luckey, & Helland, 2002; Paulsen & Feldman, 1995). Indeed, Park and Braxton (2013) find that faculty members at 4-year colleges and universities tend to be involved across the four domains. Using data on faculty behaviors reflective of Boyer's four domains of scholarship, the authors empirically delineate immersed scholars, localized scholars, scholars of engagement, scholars of pedagogical practice, and scholars of dissemination—all of which cut across at least two of Boyer's four domains of scholarship. The purpose of this chapter is to investigate whether similar patterns of involvement across Boyer's domains exist in a different and rapidly expanding component of American higher education: community colleges.

We assert that the justification for such an investigation stems from the findings of recent research by Braxton and Lyken-Segosebe (Chapter 1) on the engagement of community college faculty in scholarship reflective of Boyer's four domains of scholarship. From a national sample of faculty holding full-time positions in community colleges, Braxton and Lyken-Segosebe learned that community college faculty exhibit varying degrees of engagement in Boyer's four domains of scholarship. With publications used as an index of engagement in scholarship, Braxton and Lyken-Segosebe found

NEW DIRECTIONS FOR COMMUNITY COLLEGES, no. 171, Fall 2015 © 2015 Wiley Periodicals, Inc.
Published online in Wiley Online Library (wileyonlinelibrary.com) • DOI: 10.1002/cc.20151

that more than two fifths (43.7%) of community college faculty members have published one to two times within the past 3 years scholarship reflective of Boyer's domain of the scholarship of integration. However, they also found that the vast majority of community college faculty members have no publications in the past 3 years associated with the scholarship domains of application, discovery, and teaching (Chapter 1). In contrast, a different picture emerges when Braxton and Lyken-Segosebe used unpublished but publicly observable outcomes of scholarship as an indicator of engagement in scholarship. They found that the majority of community college faculty members produced one to two times unpublished outcomes of scholarship associated with the domains of application (70.7%) and of integration (57.1%) and that more than half (51.3%) of community college faculty members produced three to five times during the past 3 years forms of unpublished outcomes of scholarship associated with the scholarship of teaching (see Chapter 1).

Given this pattern of findings, we seek herein to better understand faculty engagement in scholarship at community colleges and investigate how scholarly types of faculty members may emerge across Boyer's domains of scholarship. Specifically, we ask: Do the behaviors and activities of community faculty members tend to cluster in patterns cutting across Boyer's four domains of scholarship? We describe the methods and analyses we used to address this question in the appendix to this volume.

Findings

We empirically identified three types of community college faculty members: Immersed Scholars, Scholars of Dissemination, and Scholars of Pedagogical Knowledge. Table A.4 displays the results of the cluster analysis that provides the basis for the delineation of these three types of community college scholars. Immersed Scholars are involved in all four of Boyer's domains. In terms of scholarship behaviors, Immersed Scholars show more involvement than their peers in such activities as developing examples to help students learn, trying new instructional practices, conducting seminars for lay people and local high schools, as well as presenting papers at a scholarly meeting. As indicated by Table A.3, Immersed Scholars tend to be more predominantly found in the natural sciences, hold the rank of full professor, and have earned a doctorate degree. This type of community college faculty scholar comprises 31% of the sample of community college faculty members described in the appendix.

Scholars of Dissemination seek to share their knowledge and research with a broader community. These scholars are involved in such activities as developing a collection of teaching resource materials, lecturing in a colleague's class, and developing new processes for dealing with practice. As suggested by Table A.3, Scholars of Dissemination, compared to their peers, are more likely to be found in sociology departments; hold a more junior, untenured rank; and are split nearly equally between faculty holding doctorates versus master's degrees. This type of community college faculty scholar encompasses 47% of the sample of community college faculty members described in the appendix.

Scholars of Pedagogical Practice, in comparison to their peers, are more heavily involved in such activities as developing examples to help students learn, experimenting with new teaching methods, and creating new approaches for class-management and examination practices—Scholars of Pedagogical Practices are most heavily involved in Boyer's scholarship of teaching. These scholars are distributed across the four disciplines in much the same way as the overall sample of community college faculty described in the appendix, with a slightly greater percentage of faculty members being housed in the history department. The same parallel to the sample distribution is also true with respect to academic rank, with a slight increase in the percentage of assistant professors and decrease in the percentage of instructors. Scholars of Pedagogical Practice are just as likely to hold doctorate degrees as they are master's degrees yet are less likely to be White than the other two types of community college faculty scholars. This type of community college faculty scholar involves 22% of the sample—the smallest of the three types of faculty scholars. Table A.3 supports these assertions.

Discussion and a Recommendation

Through our analysis, we identify three clusters of faculty members: Immersed Scholars, Scholars of Dissemination, and Scholars of Pedagogical Practice. At the broadest level, however, we observe that faculty activities within all three clusters and, indeed, as defined by all poles of the discriminant analysis function contain one common theme: an emphasis on teaching. In contrast, only immersed scholars show significant involvement in the scholarship of discovery. These findings are perhaps not surprising given the historical mission of community colleges with a strong emphasis on teaching. What may be surprising to some, however, is the extent to which community college faculty and particularly the Immersed Scholars (nearly one third of the sample) are engaged in all four of Boyer's domains, including the scholarship of discovery.

The findings from this study yield some contrasts, yet with some similarities, to previous work by Park and Braxton (2013) at a 4-year institution that identified five clusters of faculty members: Immersed Scholars, Localized Scholars, Scholars of Engagement, Scholars of Pedagogical Practice, and Scholars of Dissemination. Although we identified only three types of community college scholars, all three of these types of scholars also exist in 4-year colleges and universities (Park & Braxton, 2013), suggesting that faculty behaviors may not be as different in some ways between 2-year and 4-year institutions. Of note, however, is that we failed to identify Localized Scholars or Scholars of Engagement in 2-year colleges. One possible explanation for this finding could be tied to the historical mission of community colleges. Localized Scholars at 4-year institutions were defined as scholars who were more likely to engage in such activities as giving public talks and/or conducting research for local organizations. Although not definitive of any one cluster, we do see these activities emerge across the entire faculty in the community college sample, suggesting that although specific Localized Scholars may not exist at a community college, perhaps there is a general pervasiveness among all community college faculty to serve their local community. The same could be said of Scholars of Engagement, which were defined in the 4-year study as faculty members who strive to produce scholarship related to both theory and practice. In the community college analysis, research appears to be connected tightly to the desire to serve both theory and practice.

Nevertheless, Localized Scholars as a distinct type of faculty scholar should exist in community colleges given that community service has historically been identified as part of the mission of the community college. In his 1969 book, *The Community Dimension of the Community College,* Ervin Harlacher recognized that ever since 1945 when the community services function became part of its mission, the community college has been obligated to contribute to the intellectual life of the college district community and provide the community with the leadership and coordination capabilities of the college, assist the community in long-range planning, and join with individuals and groups in attacking unsolved problems. According to Harlacher, the community college is required to "utilize its catalytic capabilities to assist its community in the solution of basic educational, economic, political, and social problems" (p. 90). Although community college administrators and staff members bear some of this responsibility to the local context, community college faculty members also share responsibility for serving the community in some of these ways. In particular, Localized Scholars could shoulder such a responsibility given that they hold a strong sense of duty to their local communities (Park & Braxton, 2013). Policies and practices of individual community colleges should work to encourage the development of Localized Scholars as a type of faculty scholar at their institution. In Chapter 7, Braxton, Doyle, and Lyken-Segosebe outline some ways in which community colleges can foster the engagement of some of their faculty members in scholarship.

Conclusion

This chapter has investigated patterns of scholarly activities of community college faculty members, identifying three types of faculty: immersed scholars, scholars of dissemination, and scholars of pedagogical practice. These patterns have both similarities and differences with earlier work conducted among faculty at 4-year institutions. The differences that emerge between sectors appear to mirror the historic mission of the community college—to serve and support the local community. Although we have unearthed definite patterns in faculty behaviors, one remaining question is how these behaviors are rewarded by the faculty members' institutions. In a review of the literature on faculty reward structures, Park (2011) identifies a number of ways in which faculty reward structures may not be fully aligned with Boyer's four domains of scholarship. As we identify clusters of scholarship where some appear to cut across Boyer's four domains whereas others may be focused on only one domain, future research is warranted on how the three types of faculty are rewarded within their institutions and whether rewards are reaped differentially by the three clusters of faculty we identify. Although this question remains unanswered for now, it is clear that faculty behaviors at community colleges tend to cluster into distinct groups and that reward structures that equitably distribute benefits to these different types of clusters appear to be warranted.

References

Boyer, E. L. (1990). *Scholarship reconsidered: Priorities of the professoriate*. Princeton, NJ: Carnegie Foundation for the Advancement of Teaching.

Braxton, J. M., Luckey, W., & Helland, P. (2002). *Institutionalizing a broader view of scholarship through Boyer's four domains*. Hoboken, NJ: Jossey-Bass.

Glassick, C. E., Huber, M. T., & Maeroff, G. I. (1997). *Scholarship assessed: Evaluation of the professoriate*. San Francisco, CA: Jossey-Bass.

Harlacher, E. L. (1969). *The community dimension of the community college*. Englewood Cliffs, NJ: Prentice-Hall.

Park, T. J. (2011). Do faculty members get what they deserve? *Journal of the Professoriate*, 6(1), 28–47.

Park, T. J., & Braxton, J. M. (2013). Delineating scholarly types of college and university faculty members. *Journal of Higher Education*, 84(3), 301–328.

Paulsen, M. B., & Feldman, K. A. (1995). Toward a reconceptualization of scholarship: A human action system with functional imperatives. *Journal of Higher Education*, 66(6), 615–640.

Shulman, L. S., & Hutchings, P. (1998). *About the scholarship of teaching and learning: The Pew scholars national fellowship program*. Menlo Park, CA: The Carnegie Foundation for the Advancement of Teaching.

TOBY J. PARK *is an assistant professor of economics of education and education policy at Florida State University.*

JOHN M. BRAXTON *is a professor of education in the Higher Education Leadership and Policy Program at Peabody College of Vanderbilt University.*

DAWN LYKEN-SEGOSEBE *received her PhD in leadership and policy studies from Vanderbilt University.*

This chapter looks at community college faculty engagement in scholarship. Community college faculty spend the majority of their time engaged in teaching, and therefore their scholarship typically focuses on strengthening curriculum and instruction. The paper identifies some of the structural and cultural challenges and supports to scholarship at community colleges. The author concludes that mechanisms for encouraging and rewarding scholarship at community colleges remain underutilized.

Faculty Scholarship at Community Colleges: Culture, Institutional Structures, and Socialization

Vanessa Smith Morest

Approximately one third (28%) of all postsecondary 2- and 4-year faculty[1] are employed at public community colleges. The vast majority (70%) of community college faculty are part time, resulting in a relatively small number (approximately 112,000) of full-time community college faculty nationwide (Knapp, Kelly-Reid, & Ginder, 2010). Unlike the full-time faculty of 4-year colleges and universities, the community college faculty workload unambiguously places a priority on teaching. This heavy emphasis on teaching presents both opportunities and challenges. On one hand, it allows faculty to focus their work on fewer activities, presumably maximizing the amount of time spent working with students. On the other hand, less time is available to invest in scholarship. An expanded role of community college faculty in scholarship could potentially contribute to stronger teaching and increased legitimacy of community colleges. This chapter explores the perspective that although external forces may provide support for scholarship, internal structures of community colleges make it difficult for faculty to engage in scholarship.

Despite the fact that community college faculty devote most of their workload to classroom teaching, scholarly activities, as defined by Boyer's (1990) four domains, do exist at community colleges. Aside from research, which is rare but not completely unheard of at community colleges, faculty members engage in practices aimed at improving teaching and developing curriculum, providing scholarly service to the college and community, and engaging with professional organizations. Increasing the role of community college faculty in scholarship requires policies and structures that support and reward these efforts. A small number of colleges have found ways to accomplish this, but widespread adoption will require external organizations, such as those preparing master's degree-level graduates, professional associations, and policy makers to create the structures that can bring about large-scale change. This chapter seeks to identify the forces that foster or impede the development of institutional cultures supportive of community college faculty engagement in scholarship.

Background

Knowledge development regarding scholarship has been influenced by the historical shift in faculty work from teaching to research (Middaugh, 2001). Until World War II, college faculty across all postsecondary sectors were predominantly engaged in teaching. With the onset of the war, institutions gained access to federal funds for research, which contributed to the growth of graduate programs. Research being conducted by faculty at a few select institutions begot an expansion of this aspect of faculty work, because graduate students entered into teaching with high levels of training and interest in research. Ultimately, this resulted in a class of universities having research as a major faculty role.

The daily work of community college faculty, and arguably the majority of 4-year faculty, did not get swept up in this progression. Nevertheless, stratification does have implications for the sector, as the emphasis on research as evidence of faculty productivity overshadows the other domains of faculty scholarship. Rather tellingly, Middaugh's (2001) description of faculty work prior to the World War II boom in research could accurately describe the basic structures of today's full-time community college faculty work:

> The faculty member, more often than not, began and ended a career at the same institution. Faculty compensation lagged well behind that for others with postgraduate degrees. In return for the less-than-competitive paycheck and unquestioned commitment to the institution, faculty were given total autonomy over their out-of-classroom activity. At the same time, following a probationary period of employment, faculty were granted tenure, that is a guarantee of lifetime employment at their institution. (p. 8)

This apparently outdated role presents a challenge to understanding the scholarship of community college faculty and has real implications for students who begin their academic careers at community colleges. The problem, defined by Boyer (1990) in his influential report prepared for the

Carnegie Foundation, is that "basic research has come to be viewed as the first and most essential form of scholarly activity, with other functions flowing from it" (p. 15).

The work of community college faculty receives relatively little attention in the literature. For example, Murray (2013) finds that, of 14 books on college faculty published from 1998 to 2013, only nine discuss community college faculty and six of these nine devote less than 5% of their pages to the topic. The thrust of the literature on community college faculty acknowledges this lack of attention, including important contributions such as *Honored But Invisible* (Grubb, 1999) and *Community College Faculty: Overlooked and Undervalued* (Townsend & Twombly, 2007).

The limited knowledge base on community college faculty complicates the process of understanding the quality and quantity of scholarly activity. However, Boyer's four domains of scholarship provide a useful framework for analyzing the community college faculty scholarship (Boyer, 1990). These domains are (a) discovery, which includes research; (b) integration, which speaks to new insights and perspectives generated through systematic interdisciplinary work; (c) application, which involves applying disciplinary knowledge to help address societal and institutional problems; and (d) teaching, which includes depth of knowledge in a specified areas as well as the ability to transfer knowledge and generate learning in students. The relative emphasis on the four domains of discovery, integration, application, and teaching varies significantly among sectors of higher education (Braxton, Luckey, & Helland, 2002). In Chapter 1, Braxton and Lyken-Segosebe focus specifically on the engagement of community college faculty in Boyer's four domains of scholarship.

Boyer's domains are helpful in understanding how faculty productivity can be measured. At 4-year colleges and universities, the primary mechanisms for assessing faculty productivity are heavily focused on the discovery domain. The process of peer review, number of publications, and the types of publications all provide evidence of the impacts of research on scientific knowledge development. Braxton and Del Favero (2002) refer to this as the traditional template for assessing faculty scholarship. Despite the presence of these measures at the center of hiring, promotion, and tenure, research suggests that many postsecondary faculty publish relatively little (Middaugh, 2001). This suggests that the role of "teaching faculty" extends far beyond the community college sector. National Study of Postsecondary Faculty (NSOPF:04) data indicated that the average community college faculty member had published less than one article in a refereed or nonrefereed journal in the last 2 years (Rosser & Townsend, 2006).

The lack of attention paid to evaluating productivity in teaching, integration, and application has consequences for community college faculty. Despite the fact that community college faculty work is heavily focused in the areas of teaching and application, methods of assessing productivity in these areas remain weak. Few community colleges have tackled this problem, leaving important opportunities for peer review and evaluation out of the organizational structure.

Community College Faculty Work

The students served by community colleges are an important factor shaping the culture of the institutions. The highly diverse makeup of community college students combined with a heavy emphasis on part-time attendance makes for challenging teaching. Before engaging in a discussion of the institutional structures surrounding scholarship, it is helpful to consider how the day-to-day work of community college teaching can itself impose on the time and energy faculty have available for scholarly activity.

As "open door" institutions that impose few limitations on individuals wishing to take classes, the students served by community colleges are diverse by almost any measure. Overall, 15% of students at community colleges are African-American and 35% of African-American postsecondary students attend community colleges. Hispanic students comprise 18% of community college students, and 47% of Hispanic postsecondary students attend community colleges (National Center for Education Statistics, 2011, Table 241). The number of Hispanic students attending community colleges has in fact been increasing steadily in recent decades (Melguizo, 2009). It is worth noting that, although the student population is highly diverse, the faculty are not. Data from the 2005 Integrated Postsecondary Education Data System dataset indicate that 82% of full-time faculty at community colleges are White, 7% are Black, non-Hispanic, and 5% are Hispanic (Townsend & Twombly, 2007). This contradiction is certainly an area that deserves more attention as it relates to teaching and learning at community colleges.

Not surprisingly, given their demographic diversity, community college students are motivated by a wide range of academic goals. Many students choose community colleges for their convenience. The colleges are known for their flexibility, offering a variety of course schedules and formats, including weekends, late at night, early in the morning, or accelerated into 2- or 3-week sessions, to name a few. This flexibility coupled with low price makes the community college attractive to students with significant responsibilities outside school, such as work and family. Students have a multiplicity of goals (Bailey, Jenkins, & Leinbach, 2005; Cohen & Brawer, 2009). Although some students seek only a course or two from the community college, others wish to complete a degree or to transfer. Two thirds of community college students attend part time, sometimes enrolling in only one or two courses at a time and therefore requiring more than 4 years to complete a 2-year degree.

This is the milieu that frames faculty scholarship at community colleges. The number of hours spent in the classroom combined with the heterogeneity of students needs leave faculty with little discretionary time for scholarship. This assertion is supported by the results of the Community College Faculty Survey of Student Engagement (CCFSSE), which captures some information about faculty work.[2] The fall 2013 administration included 36,896 faculty at 113 institutions. Respondents are equally split between full- and part-time faculty. The results are consistent with the research on community college faculty, in that faculty spend a great deal of time teaching and engaged in service or administrative work.

Forty-eight percent of full-time faculty typically spend 13 to 20 hours teaching in class each week. There is considerable repetition in community college teaching, as 59% of full-time faculty report teaching the course in which they are being surveyed 10 or more times. This is also true of 36% of the part-time faculty surveyed. Most faculty report spending only 1 to 4 hours weekly on research and scholarly activities. Among full-time faculty, 88% report spending 1 or more hours a week on committee work and 73% spend 1 or more hours on coordination or administrative work. Participation in practices associated with the scholarship of teaching are low. During the current academic year, 15% of full-time faculty are engaged in team teaching, 11% are teaching linked courses, 10% are teaching in learning communities, and 13% are using service learning. Participation of adjuncts in service learning and linked classes is similar to that of full-time faculty; however, fewer are engaged in team teaching or service learning.

These results indicate that full-time faculty are spending roughly half of their working hours (assuming a 35–40 hour workweek) physically in the classroom. If one estimates a one-to-one ratio of prep time to classroom time this alone would make up the remaining work hours. However, this ratio is reduced somewhat by the fact that community college faculty teach the same courses repeatedly. Nevertheless, the potentially high volume of student work to review may mitigate this, particularly given the academic weaknesses of many community college students. Add to this the administrative work engaged in by nearly three quarters of full-time faculty, and time available for scholarship is reduced to the off-contract days of summer.

Nevertheless, there remains space for faculty to engage in scholarship within these constraints, particularly through the scholarship of teaching. However, the CCFSSE results reveal that no more than 15% of faculty reported participation in teaching oriented toward scholarly activity, including learning communities, service learning, or team teaching. Even taking into consideration the practicalities of community college teaching, a scholarly culture would contribute to higher proportions of teachers participating in the scholarship of teaching. The next section focuses on how the culture of community colleges shapes and constrains scholarly activity.

Culture, Institutional Structures, and Socialization

Few structures exist at community colleges to encourage scholarship. Faculty work tends to reflect a classic Weberian bureaucracy, which emphasizes rules and procedures, a lack of personalization, and hierarchical relationships. Although estimates vary, 60 to 90% of full-time community college faculty are represented by collective bargaining agreements of some kind (Townsend & Twombly, 2007). Faculty contracts often describe requirements for hiring, promotion, and tenure (Levin, Kater, & Wagoner, 2006) but do not specify evidence of scholarly activity. In order for a culture of scholarship to exist in the community college sector, practices must be present internal and external to the college that encourage faculty work beyond the daily tasks of classroom teaching.

Internal Influence on Scholarship. Community college faculty are hired through two distinct hiring processes, depending upon whether they are full or part time. Full-time faculty members are typically hired by committee. The makeup and methodology of these committees depend on local policy and practice. The literature suggests, however, that assessment of the teaching ability of candidates during the interview process is limited (Grubb, 1999; Murray, 2013; Twombly, 2005). Faculty often provide a 15–30 minute demonstration for search committee members along with other faculty and staff, whereas less than a third include students in this process (Murray, 2013, p. 113).

The hiring of adjunct faculty differs significantly in that search committees are not typically necessary. Hiring of part-time faculty is generally carried out by department chairs who are also the full-time faculty of the college. Because the proportion of faculty teaching full time is relatively small, many full-time faculty are also department chairs, meaning that the role of community college faculty as managers of adjunct faculty has become increasingly important. A department chair may be responsible for hiring and managing a workforce of numerous adjuncts. There is often no assessment of teaching in the hiring of adjunct faculty, with the view that teaching can be evaluated during the course of the semester and a weak adjunct need not be rehired. However, because a department chair may need to hire 10 or more faculty, it is disadvantageous to make these changes, undermining the practice of ensuring quality through short-term contracts.

The promotion and tenure process of community colleges also does not emphasize scholarship. Among unionized faculty, the length of time until promotion and tenure are part of the collective bargaining agreement. By failing to include peer review from faculty external to the institution and within the same discipline, it is difficult for promotion and tenure committees to assess faculty work except in terms of student course evaluations and service to the institution. This contributes to cultural norms at community colleges in which faculty are perceived as entitled to promotion and tenure after specified amounts of time.

The contribution of practices in hiring, promotion, and tenure to the culture of community colleges is to place a strong premium on the classroom and much less emphasis on other types of activities. The role of faculty outside the classroom tends to focus on service to the institution itself, rather than to the discipline. The heavy teaching schedule of faculty combined with limited resources for professional development further reinforces the norm of pursuing professional recognition within the institution rather than externally. These cultural norms are replicated by the senior faculty and staff on the committees evaluating new faculty, as this is the system through which they were socialized.

Researchers and organizations focused on educational reform are seeking ways to intervene in this cycle by introducing community college faculty to scholarly work. These external influences can provide incentives and peer engagement for faculty willing to undertake scholarly work.

External Influences.   Community colleges are publicly funded institutions, relying primarily on state funds and tuition for resources. Over the past decade, state funding for community colleges has declined (Mullin, 2010), which affects community college teaching in the areas of class size and institutional priorities (Grubb, 1999) as well as the prevalence of adjunct faculty (Levin, Kater, & Wagoner, 2006). As Grubb and associates observe, funding shortages result in community colleges pursuing external funds for innovation (Levin, 2001). Federal programs such as TRIO, Title III, and Title V provide millions of dollars to community colleges to restructure and innovate. Although much of this funding is spent on student services and technology, some of it is used to provide faculty with resources to innovate their curriculum and pedagogy. The past decade has seen an increased interest in community college practice overall on the part of new funders such as the National Science Foundation, the Lumina Foundation, and Bill and Melinda Gates Foundation. As a result, the availability of external funds creates a strong incentive to pursue them.

Grant funds influence community college faculty primarily through professional development and by creating time and space for scholarly work. By way of professional development, faculty are introduced to new networks of peers outside their institutions. Conferences and meetings aimed at improving curriculum or learning about new teaching techniques can offer faculty the opportunity to learn from those outside their institutions. Grant funds facilitate this by releasing faculty from some of their workload or paying faculty for work during the summer. Often, grant funds will also make it possible for faculty to share their professional development and scholarly work with others at their institutions by providing support for workshops and curriculum development.

Because grants stem from a variety of funders with different missions and perspectives and are directed toward many relatively small-scale innovations, it is difficult to track their impacts. The focus of much grant-funded work appears to be on increasing student success by way of improving advising, developing learning communities, and creating student success courses. The attention being paid to teaching and learning is less, although it is present through initiatives such as the Carnegie Foundation for the Advancement of Teaching's developmental math initiatives.[3] One impact of the external funds on faculty is that college administrators are routinely distracted by a multitude of initiatives. Writing and managing grants is a major activity of community college administrators. These grants structure the faculty's involvement in innovation. On one hand, grants create space for faculty to engage in scholarship, but on the other, the focus tends to be externally driven or defined by college administrators.

Although they are of major importance to faculty at 4-year colleges and universities, professional associations do not play a significant role in scholarship for community college faculty. This places an important limitation on the development of faculty networks and the ability of community college faculty to exchange ideas with faculty at other institutions. The results of the scholarship activities of community college faculty are less likely to be shared without a network to support communication. Communication in the form of publication, peer review, presentations, and service to the association are key structures of the scholarship. Yet, although these structures exist, few community college faculty are engaged in them.

In order to support scholarship at community colleges, major national associations have committees or interest groups devoted to community college teaching. For instance, the American Psychological Association Committee of Psychology Teachers at Community Colleges (PT@CC) had 1,421 members at the end of 2013 (APA Committee of Psychology Teachers at Community Colleges [PT@CC], 2013). The American Sociological Association has only a Taskforce on Community College Faculty in Sociology with a small membership. The American Mathematical Association of Two-Year Colleges (AMATYC) is a much larger organization, established in 1974 and currently having over 2,000 members (American Mathematical Association of Two-Year Colleges, 1999).

In the occupational degrees and certificates, professional associations may play a stronger role in guiding the scholarship of teaching than those representing the disciplines. The engagement of these professional associations is highly varied and rests largely on the accreditation process as a primary motivator in encouraging scholarship. For example, the National Association for the Education of Young Children (NAEYC) accredits early childhood programs using standards that require faculty to collect and review students' ability to reach specific learning outcomes (e.g., Standard Five: Use content knowledge to build meaningful curriculum). However, participation is not high, as there are only 158 accredited early childhood associate degree programs nationwide out of over 1,000 community colleges. Similarly, the American Bar Association (ABA) accredits paralegal programs using standards that reinforce high-quality teaching. In the state of California, there are currently 16 ABA accredited paralegal programs in the state's 112 community college. ABET accredits associate-level engineering technology programs. The National Council of State Boards of Nursing not only accredits nursing programs but also contributes to the development of evidence based nursing.[4]

These organizations can potentially play a critical role in shaping the scholarship of teaching at community colleges, by using accreditation standards to reinforce the ongoing evaluation of teaching and learning. Their conferences and publications could serve as important sources of professional development and networking for community college faculty, if institutional incentives for participation existed.

Unfortunately, the external influences described here meet with the internal practices that do not support scholarship. For instance, although faculty may be released from teaching in order to engage in scholarly work, the demand for adjunct faculty combined with low salaries may mean they are teaching overload courses or serving as adjuncts at other institutions. Or, willingness to undertake grant-funded work that has been defined by college administrators may be challenged in a unionized environment by a committee that places little value on this work. The grant funds may also simply reach too few faculty to help institutions move from innovation and early adoption into majority participation (Rogers, 2010).

Nevertheless, although community college faculty scholarship is limited in scope, there are areas of growth and high engagement that are described in the next section. The examples described reinforce the contention that factors external to community colleges lead to a supportive culture, whereas internal structures and process impede it.

Examples of Faculty Scholarship at Community Colleges

Recognizing that community college faculty lack time and structural incentives to undertake scholarship, a number of organizations seek to create external structures that will finance and support this work. The focus of much of this work is on improving student outcomes through curriculum development.

Faculty scholarship at community colleges take a number of forms. Often scholarly activities involve faculty working together both on campus and in committees that have formed regionally around a specific scholarly task. Examples might include the development of curriculum in a new area or incorporating technology into an existing curriculum. Committees are also formed as a result of state legislation. For example, developing a statewide general education core curriculum might include faculty from both 2- and 4-year colleges. In this section, I review several promising areas of community college faculty scholarship.

The Advanced Technological Education (ATE) program is funded through the National Science Foundation and was initiated by Congress in 1992 under the Scientific and Advanced Technology Act (SATA). The program expects community colleges to take the lead by partnering with 4-year colleges and universities, secondary schools, business, industry, and government to achieve the overarching goal of improving the quality and quantity of technicians prepared in science, technology, engineering,

NEW DIRECTIONS FOR COMMUNITY COLLEGES • DOI: 10.1002/cc

and mathematics (STEM). Funding streams include "program development and improvement," "curriculum and educational materials development," "professional development for educators," and "leadership capacity building for faculty." For fiscal year 2015, ATE expects to award $64 million in grants. Over the past decade, over 1,400 projects have been funded through this program, involving thousands of community college faculty.[5]

The ATE Centers form the backbone of the program. In fiscal year 2015, newly funded centers will receive anywhere from $1.6 to $4 million over 4 years to create partnerships and networks around program and curriculum development in STEM fields. Examples of ATE Centers include:

Bio-Link: Started at the City College of San Francisco in 1998 with the goal of developing a biotechnology curriculum in partnership with the University of San Francisco and biotech businesses. The center develops curriculum and provides support to bio-tech programs at community colleges across the country and runs a summer conference for bio-tech faculty.

SCATE: The South Carolina Advanced Technological Education Center–Center of Excellence has been in existence since 1996. They have developed an integrated, problem-based curriculum, collaborative teaching strategies, and extensive active learning techniques to strengthen teaching and learning in engineering technology.

BATEC: The Boston Area Advanced Technological Education Connections is focused on improving technician education in information technology. The center partners with high schools, provides professional development to hundreds of high school and community college faculty annually, and has established a "Bridge to Community College" program for adult learners that combines credit-bearing technology courses with English and mathematics tutoring and workshops on college admissions, financial aid, course registration, and advising.

The theory of action for the ATE program emphasizes networks of practitioners. Recipients of ATE funding meet annually at a national conference where they exchange ideas and learn about each other's projects.

Another major contribution to scholarship among community college faculty stems from the Carnegie Academy for the Scholarship of Teaching and Learning (CASTL), which existed from 1998 to 2009. CASTL was inspired by the work of Ernest Boyer (1990) and initiated by then Carnegie Foundation president Lee Shulman. Over the years, 158 faculty members pursued classroom research formally through the program (Hutchings, Huber, & Ciccone, 2011). Through scholarship of teaching and learning (SOTL) activities, faculty pursue action research projects in their own classroom. Using systematic research methods, they collect data and analyze their own teaching practice, seeking ways to improve student learning. As these faculty in the CASTL project moved into leadership positions, they have involved many other faculty in SOTL activities.

Although examples of SOTL at community colleges are limited, those involved have had an impact. At Middlesex Community College in Massachusetts, for example, faculty scholars are selected annually for participation in SOTL. The faculty prepare projects dealing with their own teaching through research and analysis. A critical aspect of the program involves peer review through periodic sharing of the work with other faculty. Examples of faculty projects include "Measuring the Effectiveness of Grammar in Contextual Exercises in College Writing" and "An Investigation of Changing Student Attitudes about Learning Chemistry."[6]

Valencia College in Orlando, Florida, also started a SOTL initiative in the late 1990s that has developed into a professional development program today. The college used federal Title III funds to create a system of faculty development that included SOTL. At Valencia, faculty must complete a faculty development program in order to be awarded tenure. This occurs through the Teaching and Learning Academy (TLA). The goal of the TLA is to "help tenure-track faculty develop a reflective approach to their teaching that is anchored in the tenets of action research and the essential competencies of a Valencia educator."[7] In order to earn tenure, faculty must demonstrate their mastery of the essential competencies by way of a portfolio that is reviewed by a wide range of stakeholders, including peers, department chairs, students, administrators, and employers.

Service learning provides an example of scholarly activity in the application domain of Boyer (1990). Braxton, Luckey, and Helland (2002) refer to service learning as a special case of the scholarship of application. Service learning is the practice of integrating service to the community into the curriculum in such a way that students can apply classroom learning to volunteer service. A critical element of service learning is the ability of the student to reflect upon their service in the context of the curriculum. The American Association of Community Colleges (AACC) began promoting and supporting service-learning initiatives at community colleges as far back as 1994. They estimate that 60–70% of community colleges today are embracing some form of service learning and community engagement (Jeandron & Robinson, 2010, p. 4). Civic engagement can be an important contribution of community colleges to their local communities, as many students and alumni live and work near their colleges throughout their lives.

Service learning forms a natural fit with community colleges because it is at the nexus between experiential learning and the community college ethos of democratic education. Because the majority of students entering community colleges lead hectic and challenging lives, it is critical that classroom-based activities are engaging and are valued by students. It can be difficult to find this combination in some of the lower level community college courses, because so many students enter the freshman year underprepared for college. The daily struggle of students to balance college with the rest of their lives opens up an opportunity for students to both learn from their own communities and contribute to them through their college work. However, crafting this into a valuable learning experience for students requires both teaching and disciplinary expertise.

Expanding Community College Faculty Scholarship

The tensions surrounding community college faculty scholarship differ from those of faculty at 4-year colleges and universities. At the 4-year level, an important tension involves the overemphasis on research or discovery at the expense of other domains of scholarship (Boyer, 1990). At community colleges, the focus is on teaching. In fact, for community college faculty who are invested in the scholarship domains of discovery, integration, and application, their efforts may remain unrecognized by their institution because these are not emphasized in the reward structure. Therefore, the question of balance remains an important one for community college faculty.

A second tension surrounding scholarship involves measuring productivity. Although higher education institutions have broadly adopted measures of productivity in research, there is less agreement regarding the evaluation of the other three domains of scholarship (Braxton & Del Favero, 2002; Middaugh, 2001). This presents a special challenge for community colleges, where teaching is at the forefront. The problem of evaluating teaching presents itself on multiple levels for community colleges because the majority of faculty members are unionized. The expectations for scholarship are largely defined through collective bargaining agreements, as opposed to institutions or professional associations.

A third area of tension involves the heavy reliance of community colleges on adjunct faculty. The vast majority of community college faculty members are actually part time. At community colleges, part-time faculty are used so extensively that their contribution to the institution can be as significant as that of full-time faculty. For example, it is not uncommon for adjuncts to teach two or three classes at a particular college year after year. Some adjuncts cobble together full-time schedules by working for multiple institutions. Evaluation of adjuncts is typically the purview of department chairs, suggesting that developing systems to evaluate and reward scholarly activity for more than two thirds of community college faculty would require new, potentially burdensome structures.

For example, office space, professional development funds, and release time are all minimal or nonexistent for part-time faculty. Even engaging adjuncts in more rigorous forms of peer review and evaluation is complicated as it would have implications for the workloads of full-time faculty. Increasing faculty scholarship at community colleges is therefore a complex problem that requires taking on the economics of the institutions and arguably the assumption that undergraduate education can be provided by faculty who are not engaged in scholarship.

NEW DIRECTIONS FOR COMMUNITY COLLEGES • DOI: 10.1002/cc

Influencing Faculty Culture.   Cultural change is needed in order to expand faculty scholarship at community colleges. Although empirical evidence of the quality and quantity of faculty engagement in scholarship is limited, it is clear that the structures that motivate scholarship at 4-year colleges and universities are not present at community colleges. Institutional incentives to change the status quo do not exist, because the financing and control of community colleges increasingly emphasize efficiency. The resources for bolstering and supporting scholarship currently come from outside the institutions, in the form of grants and multi-institutional initiatives. Although these forces arguably support change, there are other external forces contradicting them that have been discussed in this chapter, including limited financial support for community colleges and collective bargaining contracts that do not recognize or reward scholarly activity.

A few institutions are challenging this trend by linking scholarship to the key faculty transitions of hiring and tenure. For example, CUNY's Guttman Community College (GCC), which began admitting students in fall 2012, was developed using the research on teaching and learning. The goal in establishing the college's system of professional development involved "forging a culture that honors faculty collaboration and the complementary expertise shared among members of instructional teams" (City University of New York, 2008, p. 27). Faculty members work in instructional teams (ITs) to develop and review curriculum that affects all students at the college. This teamwork occurs during the academic year and at a special summer institute for professional development.

Cascadia Community College (CCC) in Bothell, Washington, opened its doors in 1994 and provides another example of a community college devoted to the scholarship of teaching. The college is structured around four principles based on Chickering and Gamson's Seven Principles for Good Practice in Undergraduate Education (Chickering, Gamson, & Poulsen, 1987): active learning, collaborative learning, critical thinking, and communication. More than a third of the CCC faculty hold PhDs, which is well above the national average. New faculty work with veteran faculty through the college's Teaching and Learning Academy while they are on the tenure track. Similar to GCC, faculty are grouped into interdisciplinary teams so that they are neither segregated by discipline nor isolated in their teaching practice.

Expanding faculty scholarship at existing community colleges is perceived to be more difficult than starting from scratch with a new college. This involves not only challenging established norms and retraining large numbers of faculty but also potentially dealing with some of the underlying constraints imposed by collective bargaining contracts and unhelpful organizational structures such as a heavy reliance on adjunct faculty. Nevertheless, community colleges currently find themselves at a crucial turning point because they have become of major interest to external stakeholders.

NEW DIRECTIONS FOR COMMUNITY COLLEGES • DOI: 10.1002/cc

Conclusions and Recommendations

Community colleges are not immune to the difficulties inherent in under-standing and measuring faculty scholarship occurring throughout higher education. The heavy emphasis on measuring scholarship in terms of re-search productivity, which is relatively straightforward, has resulted in an undervaluing of other forms of scholarship, including integration, appli-cation, and teaching. Community college faculty are therefore heavily in-vested in domains of scholarship for which we have little evidence of pro-ductivity. As a result, the scholarship of community college faculty remains poorly understood and possibly undervalued.

Very few institutions actually have mechanisms in place for identifying and rewarding community college faculty scholarship. The basic tenets of scholarship place high value on peer review and public sharing of the results of scholarship; however, these practices are largely absent from the commu-nity college culture. Community college faculty tend to work in isolation and with no requirement of publication for hiring, promotion, or tenure. It is therefore left to the institutions to establish norms involving scholarly activity. Several themes emerge from the institutional efforts to increase fac-ulty scholarship.

First, most institutions that engage faculty in scholarship do so through an entity within the college that is devoted to faculty professional devel-opment. Community college faculty typically hold master's or bachelor's degrees in their disciplines. Few have been trained in research as only a small percentage hold doctorates. Furthermore, theories about teaching and learning are not taught to community college faculty by graduate schools. Faculty need to have opportunities to learn about the body of research on teaching and learning if they are expected to become scholars of teaching. This can occur through a center or institute that is staffed and resourced to provide support to faculty.

Second, community colleges seeking to increase faculty scholarship tend to focus on major career transitions as a way to motivate faculty. Specif-ically, colleges can increase scholarship through the hiring process by hiring faculty who value scholarship. The tenure process provides another impor-tant opportunity for intervention. Colleges that are successful in nurturing faculty scholarship do so by mentoring faculty who are working toward tenure. Faculty may also be required to complete specific types of profes-sional development and to build portfolios in which they demonstrate the ability to evaluate and improve their own practice. It is important that col-leges consider ways to involve adjunct faculty in these processes as well.

Third, overcoming the isolation of community college faculty is a criti-cal step toward increasing scholarship. This can be difficult, because faculty carry high workloads in terms of the number of students they are teach-ing. Nevertheless, faculty learning communities, student learning commu-nities, and team teaching all offer opportunities to bring faculty into contact with each other. Faculty at 4-year institutions experience both collegiality and peer review through professional connections outside their institutions. Community college faculty are more internally focused, and therefore scholarly activities must be structured within institutions in order to have an impact on faculty work.

Although newly established community colleges have been successful in encouraging faculty scholarship, increasing scholarship across the approximately 1,000 community colleges nationwide requires a different approach. Community colleges are highly reliant upon their external environments for initiating organizational change. Efforts by funders to provide support to institutions and faculty to engage in scholarship have been successful. However, these initiatives are not typically aimed at widespread adoption within the institution, which requires reshaping the norms associated with community college faculty work.

Notes

1. Defined as "staff whose primary responsibility is instruction, research, and/or public service." Looking only at instructional staff, this number increases to 34%.
2. http://www.ccsse.org/CCFSSE/faccolleges.cfm
3. http://www.carnegiefoundation.org/developmental-math
4. https://www.ncsbn.org
5. FY 2015 Program Solicitation: http://www.nsf.gov/pubs/2014/nsf14577/nsf14577.pdf
6. https://www.middlesex.mass.edu/facultyandstaff/
7. http://valenciacollege.edu/faculty/development/tla/

References

American Mathematical Association of Two-Year Colleges. (1999). *The history of the AMATYC, 1974–1999*. Memphis, TN: AMATYC.

APA Committee of Psychology Teachers at Community Colleges (PT@CC). (2013). *2013 annual report*. Washington, DC: American Psychological Association.

Bailey, T., Jenkins, D., & Leinbach, T. (2005). *Is student success labeled institutional failure? Student goals and graduation rates in the accountability debate at community colleges* (CCRC Working Paper No. 1). New York, NY: Teachers College Columbia University.

Boyer, E. L. (1990). *Scholarship reconsidered: Priorities of the professoriate*. Princeton, NJ: The Carnegie Foundation for the Advancement of Teaching.

Braxton, J. M., & Del Favero, M. (2002). Evaluating scholarship performance: Traditional and emergent assessment templates. In C. L. Colbeck (Ed.), *New Directions for Institutional Research: No. 114. Evaluating faculty performance* (pp. 19–32). San Francisco, CA: Jossey-Bass.

Braxton, J. M., Luckey, W., & Helland, P. (2002). *Institutionalizing a broader view of scholarship through Boyer's four domains* (ASHE Higher and Adult Education Series, Volume 29, Number 2). San Francisco, CA: Jossey-Bass.

Chickering, A. W., Gamson, Z. F., & Poulsen, S. J. (1987). *Seven principles for good practice in undergraduate education*. Racine, WI: Johnson Foundation.

City University of New York. (2008). *A new community college: Concept paper*. Office of Academic Affairs. New York, NY: CUNY.

Cohen, A. M., & Brawer, F. B. (2009). *The American community college* (5th ed.). San Francisco, CA: Jossey-Bass.

Grubb, W. N. (1999). *Honored but invisible: An inside look at teaching in community colleges.* New York, NY: Routledge.

Hutchings, P., Huber, M. T., & Ciccone, A. (2011). *The scholarship of teaching and learning reconsidered: Institutional integration and impact.* San Francisco, CA: Jossey-Bass.

Jeandron, C., & Robinson, G. (2010). *Creating a climate for service learning success.* Washington, DC: American Association of Community Colleges.

Knapp, L. G., Kelly-Reid, J. E., & Ginder, S. A. (2010). *Employees in postsecondary institutions, fall 2009, and salaries of full-time instructional staff, 2009–10* (NCES 2011-150). Washington, DC: National Center for Education Statistics, U.S. Department of Education. Retrieved from https://nces.ed.gov/pubs2011/2011150.pdf

Levin, J. S. (2001). *Globalizing the community college: Strategies for change in the twenty-first century.* New York, NY: Palgrave.

Levin, J. S., Kater, S., & Wagoner, R. L. (2006). *Community college faculty: At work in the new economy.* New York, NY: Palgrave Macmillan.

Melguizo, T. (2009). Are community colleges an alternative path for Hispanic students to attain a bachelor's degree? *Teachers College Record, 111*(1), 90–123.

Middaugh, M. F. (2001). *Understanding faculty productivity: Standards and benchmarks for colleges and universities.* San Francisco, CA: Jossey-Bass.

Mullin, C. M. (2010). *Doing more with less: The inequitable funding of community colleges.* Washington, DC: American Association of Community Colleges.

Murray, J. P. (2013). The lack of intentionality in recruiting and hiring new community college faculty. *Journal of Modern Education Review, 3*(2), 108–119.

National Center for Education Statistics. (2011). *Digest of education statistics.* Washington, DC: NCES, U.S. Department of Education.

Rogers, E. M. (2010). *Diffusion of Innovations* (4th ed.). New York, NY: Simon & Schuster.

Rosser, V. J., & Townsend, B. K. (2006). Determining public 2-year college faculty's intent to leave: An empirical model. *Journal of Higher Education, 77*(1), 124–147.

Townsend, B. K., & Twombly, S. B. (2007). *Community college faculty: Overlooked and undervalued* (ASHE Higher Education Report, Volume 32, Number 6). San Francisco, CA: Jossey-Bass.

Twombly, S. (2005). Values, policies, and practices affecting the hiring process for full-time arts and sciences faculty in community colleges. *Journal of Higher Education, 76*(4), 423–447.

VANESSA SMITH MOREST is the interim dean of academic affairs at Norwalk Community College.

4

*The institutional culture of community colleges often fosters a
professional identity among faculty members that sees research,
publication, and other forms of out-of-class scholarship as
detrimental to teaching and student learning. But the professional
associations established by and for community college faculty
members in specific academic disciplines have forged a path to an
alternative professional identity that recognizes disciplinary
scholarship as an essential part of faculty work. This chapter
examines how the associations have fostered the social conditions
for the development of this alternative professional identity.*

Scholarship and the Professional Identity of Community College Faculty Members

James C. Palmer

Through professional training and subsequent enculturation in the workplace, individuals develop a sense of what their work entails and how it is appropriately carried out. Bucher and Stelling (1977) summarized the "dimensions" of professional identity, noting that over time members of a professional group coalesce around

1. a definition of the nature of the field—its boundaries, the problems with which it is concerned, and its basic tools and methods;
2. a sense of mission—i.e., beliefs about the larger social values served by the field;
3. the proper conditions for doing the work of the field;
4. the relationships which should obtain between people in the field and others with whom they interact—colleagues, clients, and workers in other fields; and
5. the relationship of the field to larger publics and institutions. (p. 27)

Although community college faculty members represent varying disciplines and therefore come to their teaching roles with different understandings of these dimensions after completing their graduate degree programs,

NEW DIRECTIONS FOR COMMUNITY COLLEGES, no. 171, Fall 2015 © 2015 Wiley Periodicals, Inc.
Published online in Wiley Online Library (wileyonlinelibrary.com) • DOI: 10.1002/cc.20153

there is considerable evidence that subsequent enculturation in the community college fosters a professional identity that eschews scholarly work beyond teaching. This can be seen in the tendency of some community college educators to associate this scholarly work with the perceived neglect of students by research-focused university professors, in the heavy teaching loads that leave limited time for work beyond instruction, and in the absence of any institutional requirements for out-of-class scholarly work (Cohen, Brawer, & Kisker, 2013; Townsend & Twombly, 2007). The result is an organizational culture that at best views scholarship as a personal and optional endeavor that faculty members can pursue if they wish and at worst as an abrogation of the institution's student-focused values. One respondent to a 1992 survey of community college faculty members captured both mindsets in an observation indicating that whereas he or she held to the former perspective, many others adhered to the latter perspective:

> Active hostility [to out-of-class scholarship] is found not only within the administration, but also among faculty members who seem to associate research and publication with all that is evil in the university system. I would not like to be forced to publish, but I am very angry at the lack of toleration for those who do. (Palmer, 1992, p. 63)

Yet despite the persistence and strength of this organizational culture, many community college faculty members continue to produce scholarly works that, while not always published in peer-reviewed journals, are subject to the critical review of peers and advance knowledge about the disciplines those faculty members teach or about the teaching of those disciplines within the community college context (Braxton & Lyken-Segosebe, Chapter 1 of this volume; Palmer, 1992). Although some of this scholarship is undoubtedly driven by personal interests independent of any concern for the larger profession (consider, for example, the artist who exhibits his or her work in the community and the historian who writes about or delivers public lectures on local history), some is also driven by an ongoing effort to forge a new professional identity around scholarly work that is of a distinct community college character and that broadens common understandings of what community college faculty members can contribute. This is particularly evident in the work of those participating in national disciplinary organizations involving community college faculty members, such as the American Mathematical Association of Two-Year Colleges (AMATYC), the Two-Year College English Association (TYCA), or the American Association of Physics Teachers (AAPT) through its Committee on Physics in Two-Year Colleges (CPTYC), which, among other responsibilities, provides "a common meeting ground and opportunities for communications for two-year college teachers of physics and astronomy" (AAPT CPTYC, n.d., para. 2). Though ignored or only cursorily mentioned in key works on community

New Directions for Community Colleges • DOI: 10.1002/cc

colleges generally or their faculty members specifically, these and other organizations like them have fostered the conditions for the creation of an alternative professional identity that is grounded in scholarship.

Acknowledging that there are other disciplinary organizations besides the three mentioned (e.g., the Community College Humanities Association, the Society for Anthropology in the Two-Year College, the Two-Year College Section of the National Association of Biology Teachers, the Community College Affinity Group within the Association of American Geographers, and the PT@CC network of the American Psychological Association's Committee of Psychology Teachers at Community Colleges), this chapter draws on the work of those three professional groups in English, mathematics, and physics to note how disciplinary societies made up of community college faculty members have forged a path to an alternative professional identity grounded in scholarship. In addition, the chapter discusses the factors that may impede or facilitate the realization of this professional identity, notes why this alternative professional identity is essential to the community college, and concludes with recommendations for actions that may further the efforts of community college faculty members who have embraced and who advocate for this professional identity.

An Alternative Path to Professional Identity

Organizations created for and by community college faculty members in specific disciplines arose during the post–World War II growth years of the community college movement. They emerged in response to the unease felt by the thousands of newly hired faculty members who were betwixt and between, finding a sense of belonging neither in the ranks of K–12 teachers nor within the university professoriate. An official history of the AMATYC (1999) noted that "a professional identity crisis developed for faculty that paralleled the lack of clarity of the role of the institution [i.e., the community college] within America's higher education system" (p. 62). The tendency of the professional identity of the faculty to be as uncertain as the nature of the newly established colleges, along with the consequences for faculty work on scholarship, was highlighted by Andelora (2007), perhaps the foremost scholar on the intersection between scholarship and faculty professional identity, in his historical account of the events between 1950 and 1990 that eventually led to the establishment of the TYCA:

> For most of the twentieth century, two-year college faculty were heir to many of the same issues of status and identity that plagued their institutions. Because the majority of two-year colleges were under the control of local secondary-school districts—and faculty and administrators were often hired from local secondary schools—the professional identity of two-year college faculty was tied more closely to their local communities than

to the disciplinary communities or professional organizations of their university colleagues. Not surprisingly—especially given their institutions' teaching mission—it wasn't uncommon for a two-year college faculty, over time to lose touch with scholarship, the currency of the discipline. (p. 6)

It was this identity crisis that the professional organizations addressed. Over the years they have provided a professional home for thousands of community college faculty members and, as a consequence, acted as important social settings—besides the institution itself—for professional identity formation. Their emphasis on scholarship has helped tie that identity to scholarly work in ways that counteract the predominant picture of community college faculty members as educators who are untethered from their disciplines and uninterested in extending their work beyond the classroom. This is evident in the papers delivered by community college faculty members at conferences convened by these organizations (e.g., AAPT CPTYC, 2010; AMATYC, 2014; National Council of Teachers of English, 2014), in the contributions community college faculty members have made to occasional reports published by these organizations on instructional programming within specific disciplines (e.g., Monroe, O'Kuma, & Hein, 2005), and in the articles community college faculty members have published in the newsletters and journals supported by these organizations, including the *AMATYC News*, the *MathAMATYC Educator*, and *Teaching English in the Two-Year College*. The wide-ranging character of the work published through these venues reflects Vaughan's (1997) definition of scholarship, which does not impose the singular research focus of the university on community college faculty members:

> Scholarship is a systematic pursuit of a topic, an objective, rational inquiry that involves critical analysis. It requires the precise observation, organization, and recording of information.... Scholarship is the umbrella under which research falls, for research is but one form of scholarship. Scholarship results in a product that is shared with others and that is subject to the criticism of individuals qualified to judge the product. ("Scholarship Defined" section, para. 2)

These conference papers and publications are the outward manifestation of three major achievements that have fostered the social conditions for the development of a professional identity built around disciplinary scholarship. First, the regional and national meetings of disciplinary organizations have provided venues for interaction with faculty colleagues at other community colleges, mitigating against the tendency to work in isolation without benefitting from the insights of others who face the same challenges. It was this concern for the ill effects of isolation that led community college physics instructors within the AAPT to establish the Two-Year Colleges in the 21st Century (TYC21) networking initiative, a project undertaken with funding from the National Science Foundation from 1995 through 2000 and which is now carried out in the work of the AAPT's CPTYC. Through newsletters and regional and national meetings, the TYC21 project sought to connect community college physics teachers with other community college physics teachers, creating professional networks that these educators often lacked (Monroe, Enger, & O'Kuma, 2000) and that facilitated ongoing professional communications focused on the teaching of physics at community colleges. This opportunity for networking among community college faculty members outside of their own institutions is an obvious but extremely important feature of all the disciplinary organizations, allowing faculty members to expand the circle of professional colleagues beyond the confines of their own institutions.

Second, the professional organizations have been able to create a community college presence within national disciplinary groups that are often dominated by university scholars or by educators at the K–12 level. For example, the TYCA is "an association within the Two-Year College, Four-Year College and University Section ... of the National Council of Teachers of English" (Two-Year College English Association, 2012, p. 1); the TYC21 networking efforts, as noted previously, were funded by the National Science Foundation and administered as a project of the AAPT; and the AMATYC, though an independent organization, "cooperates with the Mathematical Association of America ..., the National Council of Teachers of Mathematics ..., the American Statistical Association ..., the American Association of Community Colleges ..., Mu Alpha Theta ..., and other professional organizations" (AMATYC, n.d., para. 3). These connections address a second dimension of the isolation problem previously noted: the "estrangement" of faculty members "from their disciplines" (Andelora, 2005, p. 309), a problem that the limited networking opportunities available to community college faculty members only exacerbated (Monroe et al., 2000).

Finally, in addition to providing community college educators with a voice in their academic disciplines, these organizations have begun to establish inquiry into education at the community colleges as a legitimate and important line of scholarship that advances those disciplines, and they have championed and facilitated the role of community college faculty members as leaders in this scholarly work. Members of the TYCA, for example, have combatted the tendency of the field of writing composition to be "theorized [by university scholars] without attention to community college writing programs," a tendency that overlooks the fact that "community colleges are such critical sites for studying composition" because "there is simply no other site where the issues, complexities, and politics facing the teaching of composition are so well represented," and because the writing teachers at those institutions "have a wealth of pedagogical experience that is probably unrivaled in the university" (Andelora, 2005, pp. 317–318). The sense that attention to the community college can advance an understanding of physics education similarly drove the thinking of those leading the TYC21 networking initiative, especially in light of data showing the large proportion of undergraduate students who are introduced to science generally and physics specifically at community colleges (Monroe et al., 2000). Projects emanating from the TYC21 effort in the subsequent work of AAPT's CPTYC include *Guidelines for Two-Year College Physics Programs* that were developed by community college physics instructors drawing on their experience as 2-year college physicists (AAPT, 2002). In the field of mathematics, members of the AMATYC have similarly drawn on their expertise as mathematics educators at the lower division to take a leadership role in establishing standards for introductory college mathematics (Blair, 2006; Cohen, 1995).

These accomplishments have not been achieved with equal ease or effectiveness across disciplines. Nor have they totally overcome the reluctance of many faculty members to engage in scholarly work outside of teaching, the considerable barriers to this scholarly work that community college faculty members face (such as high teaching loads), or the dominance of university scholars in the status hierarchy of the academy. But by connecting community college faculty members with colleagues across the country, establishing a community college foothold in larger disciplinary communities, and turning the attention of those communities to the value of community colleges as venues for researching and improving undergraduate education in the disciplines, these organizations have forged an alternative route to the professional identity of community college faculty members, one that has the potential to compete with the process of enculturation that reinforces a false divide between teaching and other forms of scholarship. As Andelora (2005) noted, the efforts of community college English composition faculty members to promote published scholarship as a legitimate professional endeavor and encourage increased study of 2-year college writing programs were no less than "a campaign to rewrite" the professional identity of the faculty "in defiance of our institutional culture" (p. 308).

Barriers and Facilitators

That the disciplinary associations have endured and established themselves over time is all the more remarkable in light of the considerable obstacles still faced by those who would make scholarship a fundamental part of faculty work at community colleges. In addition to heavy teaching loads and the tenacious hold of the current institutional culture, these obstacles include attitudinal, economic, and social phenomena that limit institutional support for scholarship and work against the development of a professional identity based on scholarly work. Attitudinal barriers are evident in skepticism of the usefulness of most faculty research generally, even at universities (e.g., Bauerlein, Gad-el-Hak, Grody, McKelvey, & Trimble, 2010). The perennial concern that most research serves little more beyond the promotion of faculty careers underscores the fact that the resistance of the community college culture to enhanced faculty roles in scholarship is not solely a feature of the community college itself, but a reflection of the ambivalence with which faculty research is held both in the academy and in the larger society. Economic barriers are evident in the now-40-year history of attenuated and unpredictable state funding streams to community colleges (Palmer, 2013), which has focused the attention of administrators on cost cutting and consequently made it difficult for colleges to fiscally support faculty scholarship through released time from teaching or other measures—especially in light of the skepticism (mentioned previously) with which research is viewed. Social barriers are evident in what Levin, Kater, and Wagoner (2006) have characterized as the "corporatism and neo-liberal ideology" that has influenced contemporary public higher education policy, diminishing "the role of [the] faculty member as [an] autonomous professional" and increasing institutional reliance on a contingent workforce of part-time instructors (p. 115). As a result, the "expertise and professional judgment [of the faculty] are discounted" (p. 138), diminishing the view of faculty members as professionals with something to contribute.

These barriers, especially those posed by the neoliberal tendencies outlined by Levin et al., constitute a considerable counterforce to the work of the disciplinary organizations that have established a foothold for scholarship in the professional identity of community college faculty members. Yet in addition to commitment of the community college faculty members who take it upon themselves to establish disciplinary organizations, two countervailing forces have the potential to promote and sustain faculty scholarship. One is the commitment of many scholars outside of the community college world who recognize the importance of bringing a community college voice into regional and national conversations about undergraduate education. Indeed, the TYC21 networking initiative was undertaken with support of the AAPT, and the TYCA is affiliated with the National Council of Teachers of English. The efforts of community college faculty members to become full and respected members of professional disciplinary communities have not been easy; for example, Andelora (2005) noted that the attempts of English faculty members to establish themselves as "viable members of the discipline with a voice that would help shape the future of composition studies" has been a continuing "struggle" (p. 308). But the support of those communities, if only through a willingness to house and support community college subgroups within the larger professional associations, speaks to the presence of allies who can be helpful to community college colleagues.

A second countervailing force is the support of community college leaders who value the role of the faculty as a professional collective that is crucial to the college and its students. The extent of this leadership support across institutions has not been systematically studied, though the published observations of individual faculty members suggest that it plays out differently across institutions. In an essay titled "The End of the Community College English Profession," Kroll (2012) painted a grim picture of the declining fortunes of the faculty at his community college, arguing that the neoliberal culture described by Levin et al. (2006) had taken hold of the college with the result that faculty input in governance had been discounted and the role of faculty had been relegated to job skills training that was increasingly carried out by part-time instructors. Within the English Department, he maintained, the goal of training students in the "practical skills" and "mechanical processes" demanded by employers had displaced the goal of helping students grow and develop as writers who can, through writing, gain an understanding of themselves and the society they live in (Kroll, 2012, pp. 122–123). Responding to Kroll, Andelora (2013) acknowledged the increased emphasis on employment preparation but offered a counterpoint to Kroll's "dystopia" (p. 302) in the steps taken by his college's administration—in cooperation with the faculty—to preserve and even increase full-time faculty slots. Clearly, more research is needed on the role of top administrators in supporting and sustaining the work of a full-time professoriate, including its scholarly contributions. The lack of institutional support for scholarship remains a challenge (Andelora, 2005). But this support, where it exists, can be critical in encouraging and celebrating the work of faculty scholars.

What Is at Stake?

The continued development of the alternative path to a professional identity forged by the community college disciplinary organizations will depend primarily—as it always has—on the efforts of community college faculty members themselves. Faculty advocacy for scholarship in such documents as the TYCA's position statement on *Research and Scholarship in the Two-Year College* (TYCA, 2010) will be essential, dispelling the misconception that community college educators hold no interest in scholarly work and emphasizing a professional identity that is focused both outward toward the larger discipline as well as inward toward the classroom and the teaching mission of the institution. In terms of the framework developed by Bucher and Stelling (1977) and summarized at the beginning of this chapter, this professional identity views undergraduate teaching—the field in which community college faculty members are involved—as the purview of disciplinary scholars (e.g., English composition scholars, physicists, mathematicians) who study the problems and methods of teaching through the lens of the discipline being taught. It also embraces a professional mission of contributing to conversations about teaching within the discipline through publication or conference presentations, emphasizes the importance of institutional support for and recognition of scholarship as essential for carrying out the work of community college teaching, and underscores the critical role that relationships with disciplinary scholars nationwide play in sustaining and strengthening faculty careers.

Much of this runs counter to the notion of a community college teaching profession that is tightly bounded within the classroom and supported primarily through college-sponsored faculty development programs focusing on instructional techniques. But in addition to the advocacy of community college faculty members themselves, the alternative pathway deserves the support of university scholars, college leaders, and others concerned with community colleges and their students, because a faculty unengaged in scholarship is detrimental to the institution and to higher education generally in many respects, not just to the faculty members themselves. This disengagement reduces teaching to a process of simply "brokering information" (Vaughan, 1997, "Benefits of Scholarship" section, para. 2), denying students the opportunity to study with instructors who are actively engaged in the formation of knowledge—in the discipline, in pedagogy, or in both. It diminishes the community college voice in professional societies devoted to academic disciplines, thereby impoverishing our understanding of undergraduate education in those disciplines, especially within the context of the open-access institution and its many high-risk students. It also mutes the voice of community college faculty members in ongoing debates about higher education policy, a voice that could otherwise explain to the public what it is community college faculty members do and how that work belies the technocratic assumptions of neoliberalism (Andelora, 2013). And it sustains faculty isolation from disciplinary colleagues at both 2-year and 4-year colleges, thereby denying faculty members—and their students—the learning that derives from professional networking. Andelora (2005) put it succinctly: "Ultimately, if faculty stay divorced from their disciplines for too long, it becomes increasingly difficult for them to meet the needs of their students" (p. 315).

Supporting and furthering the groundwork laid by community college scholars through their professional organizations will require a three-pronged effort. First, the larger professional associations representing academic disciplines should continue to welcome community college colleagues and the perspectives they bring to discussions of how those disciplines can be taught and made meaningful to students. After all, community college faculty members introduce large proportions—perhaps the majority—of American undergraduates to the academic disciplines. What these students know about those disciplines, whether they go on to major in those particular disciplines or not, depends heavily on these community college educators. Initiatives supporting their involvement in the larger scholarly communities representing those disciplines will be essential. A recent example is the 2012 creation of a Task Force on Community College Faculty by the American Sociological Association (ASA). The task force is cochaired by a community college sociology professor and a community college president with a sociology background. As explained in a special issue of ASA's *The American Sociologist* edited by the cochairs and devoted to community colleges, the purpose of the task force is to

> examine the professional role, professional development, and potential advocacy needs of sociologists who are community college faculty. The task force has been charged with developing recommendations for how the ASA, as the national association for sociology, can best support community college faculty in the discipline. (Vitullo & Spalter-Roth, 2013, p. 361)

Similar task forces have been established by the American Chemical Society (n.d.) and the American Historical Association (Doyle & Cody, 2013).

In addition, faculty scholarship should be highlighted and studied by university scholars who write about the community college enterprise. Qualitative studies could complement the occasional analyses that have appeared on the quantity and types of scholarly products produced by community college faculty members. For example, researchers could conduct case studies of how faculty members persevere in scholarly work despite heavy teaching loads and limited institutional support, how the attitudes and support of college leaders factor into this scholarly work, how work on scholarly products affects their teaching, and how this work ultimately affects the formation of a professional identity. Investigations into the interactions community college faculty members have with university colleagues in national organizations representing their disciplines will also be helpful. These sorts of case studies will advance our understanding of an important aspect of faculty life that garners little attention in published scholarship on the community college, and they could offer opportunities for collaborative research involving university and community college colleagues.

Finally, and perhaps most importantly, a voice for scholarship emanating from the top community college leadership is especially needed, lending visibility to scholarly accomplishments that too often go unacknowledged and helping to make scholarship an accepted part of the community college enterprise. The work of George Vaughan (1988, 1997) who, as a long-time community college president, advocated for faculty scholarship, is a model for those community college leaders today who would support the scholarly work of their faculty members. His writings conveyed not only support for this scholarship and a definition of scholarship applicable to the community college, but also clear explanations of why scholarship is important to the academic stature of community colleges, the capacity of faculty members to remain engaged in their work over the long haul, and the intellectual integrity of classroom teaching.

Though there is little evidence that Vaughan's advocacy swayed other leaders to embrace "scholarship as part of the institutional mission" (Andelora, 2005, p. 316), renewed calls for supportive leadership must be made. For it is hard to see how institutional support for scholarship, such as release time, sabbaticals, fiscal reimbursement for participation in national disciplinary organizations, or even simple recognition or appreciation of faculty scholarship can be achieved without leaders who see the connection between scholarly work and the capacity of the institution to achieve its educational mission. And it is even more difficult to understand how scholarship can take hold in the intuitional cultures of community colleges if their leaders do not themselves model scholarly behavior, as Vaughan did throughout his years as president by writing and publishing books and essays on many aspects of the community college enterprise, including the role of scholarship in those organizations. Faculty members involved in regional and national disciplinary organizations have forged a community college presence in the larger academic community, engaging in scholarly work on their own terms rather than simply pursuing a university-based publication, often in the face of limited or no institutional support. The fruition of this work and the professional identity it fosters await strong and visible advocacy from community college leaders.

References

American Association of Physics Teachers (AAPT). (2002). *Guidelines for two-year college physics programs*. Retrieved from http://aapt.org/Resources/upload/TYC Guidelines-PDF.pdf

American Association of Physics Teachers (AAPT) Committee on Physics in Two-Year Colleges (CPTYC). (n.d.). *About*. Retrieved from https://sites.google.com/a/aapt .org/comm/about

American Association of Physics Teachers (AAPT) Committee on Physics in Two-Year Colleges (CPTYC). (2010). *Past successes and future directions. National two-year college physics meeting*. Retrieved from http://www.instruction.greenriver.edu/aapt/ tyc/TandemMeeting071710.htm

American Chemical Society. (n.d.). *ACS expands Office of Two-Year Colleges*. Retrieved from   http://www.aacc.nche.edu/Resources/aaccprograms/diversity/Documents/acs _o2yc.pdf

American Mathematical Association of Two-Year Colleges (AMATYC). (n.d.). *About us*. Retrieved from http://www.amatyc.org/?page=AboutUs

American Mathematical Association of Two-Year Colleges (AMATYC). (1999). *The history of the AMATYC, 1974–1999*. Retrieved from http://c.ymcdn.com/sites/www .amatyc.org/resource/resmgr/history/amatychistory.pdf

American Mathematical Association of Two-Year Colleges (AMATYC). (2014). *2014 Nashville conference*. Retrieved from https://amatyc.site-ym.com/?page=2014 ConfHome

Andelora, J. (2005). The teacher/scholar: Reconstructing our professional identity in two-year colleges. *Teaching English in the Two-Year College, 32*, 307–322.

Andelora, J. (2007). The professionalization of two-year college English faculty: 1950-1990. *Teaching English in the Two-Year College, 35*, 6–19.

Andelora, J. (2013). Teacher/scholar/activist: A response to Keith Kroll's "The End of the Community College English Profession." *Teaching English in the Two-Year College, 40*, 302–307.

Bauerlein, M., Gad-el-Hak, M., Grody, W., McKelvey, B., & Trimble, S. W. (2010, June 13). We must stop the avalanche of low-quality research. *Chronicle of Higher Education*. Retrieved from http://chronicle.com.libproxy.lib.ilstu.edu/article/We-Must -Stop-the-Avalanche-of/65890/

Blair, R. (Ed.). (2006). *Beyond crossroads: Implementing mathematics standards in the first two years of college.* Retrieved from http://beyondcrossroads.matyc.org/doc/PDFs/BCAll.pdf

Bucher, R., & Stelling, J. G. (1977). *Becoming professional.* Beverly Hills, CA: Sage.

Cohen, A. M., Brawer, F. B., & Kisker, C. B. (2013). *The American community college* (6th ed.). San Francisco, CA: Jossey-Bass.

Cohen, D. (Ed.). (1995). *Crossroads in mathematics: Standards for introductory college mathematics before calculus.* Retrieved from http://www.amatyc.org/?page=GuidelineCrossroads

Doyle, D. A., & Cody, C. C. (2013, May). AHA releases report on two-year college faculty. *Perspectives on History.* Retrieved from http://www.historians.org/publications-and-directories/perspectives-on-history/may-2013/aha-releases-report-on-two-year-college-faculty

Kroll, K. (2012). The end of the community college English profession. *Teaching English in the Two-Year College, 40,* 118–129.

Levin, J. S., Kater, S., & Wagoner, R. L. (2006). *Community college faculty: At work in the new economy.* New York, NY: Palgrave MacMillan.

Monroe, M. B., Enger, J., & O'Kuma, T. L. (2000). Faculty isolation: A TYC21 white paper. In J. C. Palmer (Ed.), *A model for reform. Two-Year Colleges in the Twenty-First Century: Breaking down barriers (TYC21)* (pp. 65–86). College Park, MD: American Association of Physics Teachers. Retrieved from http://files.eric.ed.gov/fulltext/ED468948.pdf

Monroe, M. B., O'Kuma, T. L., & Hein, W. (2005). *Strategic programs for innovations in undergraduate physics at two year colleges: Best practices of physics programs.* Retrieved from http://www.aapt.org/Projects/upload/SPIN-UP-TYC-Booklet.pdf

National Council of Teachers of English. (2014). *TYCA regions and conferences.* Retrieved from http://www.ncte.org/tyca/regionals

Palmer, J. C. (1992). The scholarly activities of community college faculty. In J. C. Palmer & G. B. Vaughan (Eds.), *Fostering a climate for faculty scholarship at community colleges* (pp. 49–65). Washington, DC: American Association of Community and Junior Colleges. Retrieved from http://files.eric.ed.gov/fulltext/ED350048.pdf

Palmer, J. C. (2013). State fiscal support for community colleges. In J. S. Levin & S. T. Kater (Eds.), *Understanding community colleges* (pp. 171–184). New York, NY: Routledge.

Townsend, B. K., & Twombly, S. B. (2007). *Community college faculty: Overlooked and undervalued* (ASHE Higher Education Report, Volume 32, Number 6). San Francisco, CA: Jossey-Bass.

Two-Year College English Association (TYCA). (2010). *Research and scholarship in the two-year college.* Retrieved from http://www.ncte.org/library/NCTEFiles/Groups/TYCA/ResearchScholarship.pdf

Two-Year College English Association (TYCA). (2012). *Bylaws of the Two Year College English Association and the regional associations.* Retrieved from http://www.ncte.org/library/NCTEFiles/Groups/TYCA/TYCA_Bylaws_11_2012.pdf

Vaughan, G. B. (1988). Scholarship in community colleges: The path to respect. *Educational Record, 69*(2), 26–31.

Vaughan, G. B. (1997, Spring). Why scholarship? *Inquiry, 1*(1), 8–13.

Vitullo, M. W., & Spalter-Roth, R. (2013). Contests for professional status: Community college faculty in sociology. *The American Sociologist, 44,* 349–365.

JAMES C. PALMER *is a professor in the Department of Educational Administration and Foundations at Illinois State University, Normal, IL.*

Dating back to 2004, the Achieving the Dream initiative was established to promote evidence-based programs and interventions to produce and sustain student success. Achieving the Dream has created a new environment and new forms of thinking among the faculty that have spurred some to action research within their classrooms and beyond. Using three vignettes, this chapter presents how the Achieving the Dream initiative has fostered faculty research.

A National Initiative of Teaching, Researching, and Dreaming: Community College Faculty Research in "Achieving the Dream" Colleges

Linda Serra Hagedorn

Community college faculty research could be considered an oxymoron. Historically community colleges have been bastions of teaching. Instructors pride themselves on the quality of their instruction and their ability to work with a diverse group of students, some of whom may have special needs. But a major initiative established in 2004 titled *Achieving the Dream: Community Colleges Count* (AtD) has inspired some community college faculty to explore various types of inquiry with the goal of improving their classrooms *and* promoting sustainable student success. The lofty goals of AtD require the cooperation and the integration of the entire campus community, especially faculty. The design for each participating college includes putting together working teams consisting of college administrators, faculty, staff, and institutional researchers to create a campus success initiative, evaluate it, and plan the next iteration to further enhance student success. Thus, AtD has created a new environment and new forms of faculty thinking that have spurred some to action research within their classrooms and beyond. This chapter presents three vignettes of AtD colleges highlighting how the initiative influenced and encouraged faculty research.

NEW DIRECTIONS FOR COMMUNITY COLLEGES, no. 171, Fall 2015 © 2015 Wiley Periodicals, Inc.
Published online in Wiley Online Library (wileyonlinelibrary.com) • DOI: 10.1002/cc.20154

Background

It is widely known that success among community college students is problematic. There is a plethora of research and stories in the popular media that decry low graduation rates, low transfer rates, high dropout rates, and general low success among students (Complete College America, 2012; Hagedorn, Cabrera, & Prather, 2010; Hoachlander, Sikora, & Horn, 2003). However, many of the factors contributing to low success are outside of the reach of community colleges such as inadequate academic preparation, low "college knowledge" and nonacademic skills, competing obligations, and the need for remedial education (Hoachlander et al., 2003; Rath, Rock, & Laferriere, 2013).

Diversity of Learners.   Of all the variations of higher education, community colleges attract the most diverse learners (Cohen & Brawer, 2003; McClenney & Arnsparger, 2012). Compared to 4-year universities, community colleges enroll a significant proportion of the country's students of color and low-income students. They also welcome students who require developmental/remedial instruction and students with learning problems, or stated bluntly, students who would not be welcomed by the majority of the country's 4-year universities. Moreover, community colleges attract returning adults, veterans, and those balancing work and family with their studies.

Society has typically viewed community colleges as inferior to 4-year colleges and universities (Hagedorn, 2010). Community colleges have long endured being the subject of jokes and community college students and faculty have been cast as inferior to their 4-year counterparts. This reputation has angered some and brought action by others, including President Obama. Since his inauguration, President Obama has been an advocate and a promoter of the community college, proposing bills and initiatives directly tied to the country's 2-year postsecondary sector. His enthusiastic promotion of community colleges has changed the landscape and has encouraged policy makers, philanthropic funding agencies, and college faculty to see these institutions in a new and more favorable light (White House, 2014).

Accountability and Assessment.   The attention by the president and others has elicited an increased scrutiny and call for accountability by governmental entities, policy makers, accreditors, and the general public. A recent report from the National Institute for Learning Outcomes Assessment indicates that colleges of all types have increased their student assessment activities but subsequent curricular and other changes have not kept pace (Kuh, Jankowski, Ikenberry, & Kinzie, 2014). Another report defined assessment in community colleges as "fragile" (Nunley, Bers, & Manning, 2011). Only 29% of community college respondents indicated that "the primary driver for learning outcomes assessment at my institution is our faculty" (p. 17).

NEW DIRECTIONS FOR COMMUNITY COLLEGES • DOI: 10.1002/cc

The most popular national student assessment in community colleges is the Community College Survey of Student Engagement (CCSSE) administered by the Center for Community College Student Engagement at the University of Texas at Austin. The survey instrument is administered during the spring semester and is designed to be a benchmarking instrument, a diagnostic tool, and a monitoring device for student engagement, a key factor in student learning outcomes (Center for Community College Student Engagement, 2014). The institutional measures have been found to be highly correlated to learning and retention (Center for Community College Student Engagement, 2014). Participation in CCSSE has grown consistently, from 12 community colleges in 2001 to 266 in 2012, 280 in 2013, and 349 in 2014 (Center for Community College Student Engagement, 2014).

Another recent development is the Voluntary Framework for Accountability (VFA) developed by the American Association for Community Colleges (AACC) in partnership with the College Board and the Association of Community College Trustees (ACCT). The VFA is a national assessment system with a three-pronged approach that includes metrics for measures of student progress, student learning, and workforce development. According to its creators, the VFA was formed to fill the void for authentic accountability measures specifically for community colleges (VFA, n.d.). To participate in the VFA, colleges must pay a nominal fee and become a member. According to their website, about 130 colleges or districts are currently (as of 2014) members (http://vfa.aacc.nche.edu/membership/Pages/ParticipantList.aspx). Membership provides technical manuals, display tools, and information on best practices.

Achieving the Dream

Of all of the many initiatives and projects aimed at community college student success, assessment, and accountability, the largest by far is Achieving the Dream: Community College Counts. Initially funded solely through the Lumina Foundation, AtD began in 2004, with a meeting at the Lumina Foundation offices in Indianapolis to discuss a revolutionary idea—a national initiative to increase the success of community college students. In addition to several prominent community college researchers, representatives from the American Association of Community Colleges; Community College Leadership Program at the University of Texas-Austin (CCLP); Community College Research Center, Teachers College, Columbia University (CCRC); Jobs for the Future; MDC; MDRC; and Public Agenda began a series of discussions that eventually led to this giant initiative. The stated goal of AtD is "success for more community college students, especially students of color and low-income students" (Achieving the Dream, 2012).

The initiative began with a $75 million investment and a 10-year commitment by the Lumina Foundation. In AtD's 10th year, several foundations, the largest being the Gates Foundation, have joined and are supporting success initiatives at close to 200 community college campuses across 34 states (Sturgis, 2014). The initiative has recently evolved into a nonprofit organization led by a board of directors.

The AtD approach includes assigning two veteran college coaches to each college. One coach, called the leadership coach, is often a recently retired community college president or other individual with a long history of successful administration of a community college. The second coach, called a data coach, is typically someone who is data proficient and brings expertise in the area of data display and data analyses. Many of the data coaches have previous (or current) institutional research experience. The coaches work with the colleges to enact institutional reform through a five-step process: (a) leadership commitment; (b) use of data in decision making; (c) engaging stakeholders; (d) implementing, evaluating, and improving intervention strategies; and (e) creating a culture of continuous improvement (Rutschow et al., 2011). To provide evidence of student success, all AtD colleges must collect, monitor, and analyze longitudinal data pertaining to five benchmarks:

1. Complete remedial or developmental courses and progress to credit bearing courses;
2. Enroll in and complete college-level "gatekeeper" courses;
3. Complete courses, with a grade of "C" or higher;
4. Enroll term-to-term and year-to-year;
5. Earn certificates or degrees. (Rutschow et al., 2011, p. 121)

Definition of Faculty Research

The term research typically conjures up visions of sterile laboratories filled with highly trained individuals engaged in systematic investigations to find generalized truth and to establish conclusions for the betterment of humankind. Faculty members of research institutions are often recruited and promoted for their research prowess over their pedagogical skills. Although many research universities may also involve or employ undergraduates in the research enterprise, it is more typical for university research endeavors to seek a cadre of top graduate students and postdoctoral students to work alongside faculty researchers. Research universities are generally ranked and classified by the number and quality of published journal articles in peer-reviewed journals (Bell, Hill, & Lehming, 2007).

Although it has become more commonplace for other types of 4-year postsecondary institutions to also value and seek faculty who are active in research (Selingo, 2000), community college faculty are hired to be teachers and not researchers. They routinely carry heavy teaching loads, have no research expectations, have no access to highly trained graduate students, and are generally not promoted on the basis of publications or national recognition in their discipline. I offer the example of Sandhills Community College in North Carolina that publishes the typical job description for a faculty member on their website stating "participation in formal research activity is not a contractual expectation for faculty members" (Sandhills Community College, 2011, para. 2).

Amid the growing sea of published journal articles and books, it is unfortunate that many community college administrators and presidents report that the published research is not useful to them and that they find it too complex and complicated (Morest & Jenkins, 2007). In addition, community college faculty point out that the higher education literature is focused on universities and their students and has little relevance for the type of problems community colleges face and the students they serve. Rather, community colleges would benefit from practical research that is directly applicable to practice and to their current needs.

The brand of faculty research discussed in this chapter is of a different variety than that found in the higher education journals. It is in concert with Cross's (1990) definition of "any systematic inquiry designed and conducted for the purpose of increasing insight and understanding of the relationship between teaching and learning" (p. 136). The research is not necessarily replicable, inferential, or generalizable. Rather, it is often classroom based, action oriented, situated in the present, but of high value to the college and its students. An example is a faculty member who is dissatisfied with student grades and as a result makes changes in her curriculum and compares current grades with those earned by her earlier courses to verify if the changes were beneficial.

Chapter Methodology

I was among the group of researchers invited to the first AtD gathering and have been working with the initiative since its inception. I am very familiar with the AtD process, having been a data coach for six colleges for close to a decade. To identify AtD colleges where significant faculty research was being conducted, I contacted each of the 37 AtD data coaches with an explanation of the goals for this chapter and asked them to identify faculty in the colleges in which they work who were performing faculty research. Several coaches sent me recommendations. I sent each identified faculty member an e-mail detailing the purpose of the chapter and a request for an interview. An interview protocol was included in the e-mail so that the faculty member would be prepared for my questions. Based on my interviews, I selected three colleges with somewhat different approaches to faculty-led research and have included a vignette of their work. These vignettes are each based on one campus and represent only what is happening there. But in each case, the faculty research was spurred and encouraged by AtD membership.

College Vignettes

The three vignettes from Temple College, Macomb Community College, and Community College of Baltimore County follow.

Temple College—The Awakening. Temple College, located in central Texas, consists of a main campus plus three education centers located nearby. The college serves a diverse student body including many military, active as well as military family members, from nearby Fort Hood. When Temple joined AtD in 2009, it was struggling to find ways to increase student success. As a result of their AtD membership, the core team and the faculty decided upon five interventions including their signature original "Zero Week." Each semester, the week prior to the commencement of classes, the campus is buzzing with activities including financial aid counseling, placement testing, buying of books, meeting with academic counselors, and securing of parking passes. The campus is alive with special presentations and attractions for the whole family. Zero Week has become a Temple tradition that has been emulated at other AtD colleges. In addition to Zero Week, a highly successful academic intervention is focused on developmental math.

Temple has recently been designated a leader college meaning that it has demonstrated success within the designated AtD metrics and now serves as an example to other colleges in the initiative. Temple College has experienced an awakening to the world of data and faculty research due mainly to their membership in AtD. Forced to face their developmental math data on retention and success rates,[1] several faculty designed interventions and worked with institutional research (IR) to collect data and analyze the results. Believing that students would be more likely to complete the developmental sequence if they could do so in a shorter period of time, several faculty decided to experiment by offering courses in an 8-week rather than the traditional 16-week format. The concentrated format requires students to attend class four times a week. This 8-week format allows students to take two developmental courses during the 16-week academic semester. The faculty researchers, working with IR, collected data that showed that students not only earned higher grades but were also more likely to finish the courses and to take the next course in the sequence than students enrolled in the traditional schedule. Based on these findings, most sections of developmental math are now being offered in the concentrated format.

In addition, Temple's student success director, a developmental math instructor hired to oversee developmental education, basic education, and student tutoring, did her own classroom research by analyzing classroom math assessments item by item to identify patterns related to incorrect answers. Her work allowed her to pinpoint the specific areas where students were having the most difficulty. She concentrated on these areas and targeted faculty development specifically aimed at teaching these problem areas. She continues to monitor the assessments for improvement.

NEW DIRECTIONS FOR COMMUNITY COLLEGES • DOI: 10.1002/cc

Other research consists of compiling a "repeater list" or a list of the students in a course that have attempted it before and failed. The student success director explained that having that list assisted her to "give some of those students additional attention." She also distributed the list to other instructors in the division and encouraged them to also monitor student success. By following these repeaters longitudinally through their subsequent courses, instructors are seeing the results of their special attention. Using Cross's (1990) definition, this type of "systematic inquiry provided insight" into a way for faculty to identify students requiring additional attention.

Temple College has been awakened to the value of data and to using data in their decisions. Faculty report that meetings typically include the display of data or the request for it prior to making any decisions.

> I did not do these types of activities before AtD because I didn't know what resources were available to me. I didn't know what kind of data to ask for or to look for. Being on the AtD committee, I heard about the kinds of data you can get and the kind of reports you can generate. Then I attended the DREAM² conference and heard what other colleges were doing and I said, that's a good idea, we can do it here too, so I felt I had to try new ideas and to watch what the data showed. (Success Director, Temple College)

As a result of the research at Temple, faculty and staff are presented with an internal research report when they meet as a whole during the college's Zero Week (the week before classes officially meet) as well as during the college's opening convocation each semester. Although no publications have been written, the faculty have presented results at the National Institute for Staff and Organizational Development (NISOD), the Texas Community College Teachers Association (TCCTA), and AtD's DREAM conferences.

Macomb Community College—Slow and Steady.   Macomb Community College is a huge multicampus system located in the greater Detroit area. Like many large urban community colleges, the faculty are unionized. Macomb joined AtD in 2009 and recently became a leader college. But the road to change was a very slow and arduous process. Changes had to be accepted by faculty across three different campuses and also had to have the blessing of the faculty union prior to implementation. Despite the longer process, the college has its faculty research champions who have enacted change through research.

Like most community colleges, Macomb had problems getting students through the developmental math sequence. But somewhat unique, Macomb offers the associate of general studies degree that does not have a math requirement, allowing students to graduate without facing math deficits and without taking a math course. Some Macomb faculty felt that students could be more successful in life, would have better transfer options, and would be able to choose a wider range of careers if they left Macomb with the requisite math skills. A brave math faculty member designed a course that she hoped would take the fear out of mathematics while teaching students the mathematical skills they would need after they left Macomb. She designed a course titled Everyday Math. Everyday Math uses real life situations such as understanding percentages using a shopping paradigm (think 30% off of ticket price), proportionality using body mass index (BMI), and complex equations using blood alcohol computations. Gathering data that compared grades, retention, and transfer activity, it was clear that Everyday Math is beneficial for the enrolled students. Another data point is the increased number of students enrolling for the course. Based on the research results, Macomb has expanded the number of sessions of Everyday Math and has trained additional math instructors to teach it. Moreover, Macomb's chief transfer locations accept the course for college credit.

According to members of the Macomb faculty and administration, the atmosphere at Macomb has been transformed after AtD. Learning that another Michigan AtD college, Oakland Community College, had held "data summits" where data were displayed to faculty and others with the intention of encouraging positive changes, Macomb adopted the idea and now it too regularly conducts well-attended data summits where data are prominently displayed and used to answer faculty-developed questions related to student success. Moreover, such parades of data have elicited more data inquiries for local research performed by faculty in tandem with institutional research. The interest in data and local research has developed to the extent that a new position, the director of special research projects, was created due in part to manage the college's research needs.

An example can be seen from the college's accounting faculty who due to low pass rates in their gateway course were considering a screen that would set a floor math placement score for enrollment in the course. With the aid of IR, they analyzed the relationship of math placement and subsequent course success and found that the relationship was very weak. As a result, they have decided to forgo the math screening and instead try a new curriculum to help solve the problem. They will be monitoring student success to evaluate the new curriculum. This process provides a good example of classroom research per Cross (1990).

Based on faculty requests voiced at the summits, the director of special programs was directed to perform college-level research on incoming students placing into all three developmental courses (reading, math, and English). Based on the results, Macomb has now implemented a policy that incoming students requiring remediation in all areas take a student success course. This decision was based on research showing significant gains in persistence, as high as 15% to 20%, especially among African-American students, as well as evidence of higher grade point averages in the first semester among Macomb's students requiring that high level of remediation. Technically, the faculty members were not the ones who "crunched the numbers" but the research questions arose from the faculty who needed the technical assistance of the director of special programs to perform this variety of college-level institutional research.

> There is now an atmosphere here in the college and particularly with the provost that says if the data strongly suggests something then we make a change in policy. And I don't know if that would have happened if the college wasn't in the AtD initiative. But just being in that initiative in the constant production of data examination in how the interventions are working … if that hadn't taken place, I am not so sure that administration would be as willing as they are today to make changes in policy and have people implement it. When I came to the college in 2000, the college would not have dared to do something like this. (Director of Special Research Programs)

Other research requested by faculty included the relationship between reading placement score and progress in online courses, foreign language progression from level to level, and the relationship of success in science courses with math placement. Although the Macomb faculty were not the ones performing the research per se, they were awakened to the value of research and requested technical assistance by those better trained to actually perform the statistical analyses. An English faculty member summed up AtD's role this way:

> AtD was consistent with what we wanted to do and what we were doing. This type of research is part of the teaching—or at least it should be. AtD was confirming what we should be doing and gave us the opportunity to do it.

Although there have not been any formal publications related to the research at Macomb, there have been quite a few internal reports that are presented at faculty meetings and other convenings. Faculty have presented at the AtD DREAM conference. But according to one faculty member "I haven't even thought about publishing the results of our work here. … I just don't have the time."

Community College of Baltimore County (CCBC)—Weaving AtD Into Other Programs.   CCBC is a large urban community college that joined AtD in 2009. CCBC is proud of its history of faculty innovation and research. Specifically, beginning in the 1990s, Peter Adams, an English faculty member who was then the head of the writing program, started collecting data on students in developmental writing classes. He and his colleagues became concerned that students were not passing college-level English. With the aid of his Apple IIE computer, Adams tracked his students for 4 years discovering that only about one third of the students in the upper-level developmental writing course ever passed English 101 and that number was even lower for the students in the lower level (about 13%). With that, Adams and colleagues came up with an idea. What if instead of approaching developmental writing as a hurdle to get over before taking

English 101, it could become a corequisite with English 101, thus acting as an aid to accelerate students through English 101? Thus the Accelerated Learning Program (ALP) was born.

In essence, the ALP allows students who place one level below college-level writing to enroll in a special English 101 course consisting of only 20 students, 10 of whom tested into developmental writing and the other 10 already meeting the English 101 requirements. The 10 ALP students, however, also meet in a class scheduled directly after English 101 designated the ALP course—taught, in most cases, by the same instructor of English 101 and designed only for them, containing only those 10 students. Subsequent research requested by the faculty but actually performed by the college institutional research office has revealed that about two thirds of the ALP-enrolled students pass English 101. Additionally, longitudinal data revealed a doubling of the number of developmental students who also passed English 102 as well as other milestones such as completing 30 and 60 credit hours, transferring, and graduating.

After CCBC joined AtD, the Community College Research Center at Columbia University did a more sophisticated analysis of ALP verifying the positive results (Cho, Kopko, Jenkins, & Jaggars, 2012). ALP faculty agreed that although AtD cannot be credited for the ALP program, the AtD ideals supported and reinforced it. Faculty credit their AtD data coach for "going to bat for them" and convincing the IR office that English deserves priority and research support. Moreover, when CCRC verified the results, "people took greater interest."

> Data on programs like mine (ALP) were just too low of a priority until AtD. What we were doing was following students after they finished 101. But AtD gave us the kind of attention we needed so that our work roused attention. (CCBC English faculty)

CCBC faculty working in the ALP program credit AtD with "getting the word out" to other colleges in the initiative. As a result of the success of ALP, CCBC now has accelerated programs in developmental math and reading. However, CCBC wants to be clear that although AtD has supported their program, the success was also due to the hard work of a vice president in the college who supported the ALP. The ALP faculty use the term "cross-fertilization" when describing the AtD role. They discussed how AtD leadership and core team meetings not only allowed other faculty to learn more about ALP but also allowed ALP to take on new ideas. For example, hearing a discussion at an AtD team meeting on financial literacy gave ALP faculty the idea of incorporating financial topics into the writing course.

> How do we have time in 14 weeks to worry about how to get students to learn to write and then worry about how they take care of their finances or their families? So one of the things we tried to do was have the students write

papers on financial issues such as credit cards, loans, and other issues. That way they were working on their writing skills and financial literacy at the same time. All of that came out of those meetings.

Peter Adams, although now retired, still gets excited talking about ALP and how it is being scaled up and replicated at other AtD colleges. The result of ALP is that there is now a national conference, Acceleration in Developmental Education, where faculty from both community colleges and 4-year colleges present their research. The 2014 conference featured several CCBC faculty discussing the program at their college. Adams has also coauthored reports that are available through ERIC and a published article in the *Journal of Basic Writing* (Adams, Gearhart, Miller, & Roberts, 2009).

Conclusion

I conclude this chapter using Bronfenbrenner's (1979) Developmental Ecology Model to illustrate community college faculty members' development toward a culture of research and evidence. Describing a series of nested structures beginning furthest from the individual and becoming more and more proximal, Bronfenbrenner labels the systems macro-, exo-, meso-, and micro- (see Figure 5.1).

Figure 5.1. Development Spheres of AtD Community College Faculty

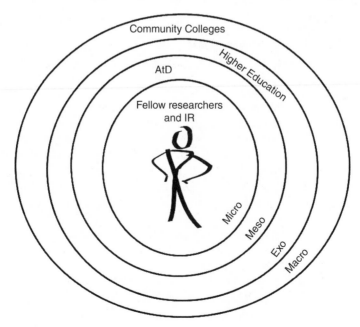

Macrosystems consist of a specific culture and environment defined by norms and expectations. For community college faculty, I have defined that system as the culture of the community college. Next comes the exosystem, defined by Bronfenbrenner (1979, 1989) as the place where the developing person's ecology links to a setting that can only be indirectly connected. For the developing faculty the exosystem consists of the culture of higher education. Although community colleges are within the sphere of higher education, for community college faculty that connection can be indirect.

In the next sphere, mesosystems are the "the interrelations among two or more settings in which the developing person actively participates" and are "formed or extended whenever the developing person moves into a new setting" (Bronfenbrenner, 1979, p. 25). This occurs when a college joins the AtD initiative and its emphasis on a culture of evidence. In the sphere closest to the community college faculty member, the microsystem represents the patterns of interactions that are directly experienced (Bronfenbrenner, 1979). This consists of fellow faculty who are also research minded as well as a relationship with the college's IR. Hence, as a result of membership within AtD some faculty members have experienced development that has transformed them and their environments to embrace a culture of evidence to enhance student success.

In this chapter I have presented three examples of colleges that due to their involvement in AtD (a mesosystem) have participated in some level of faculty research as defined by Cross (1990), a "systematic inquiry designed and conducted for the purpose of increasing insight and understanding of the relationship between teaching and learning" (p. 136). In some cases the faculty joined forces with their institutional research department because they sought data and analyses that required the assistance of others with specific expertise. But the motive remained constant: improved student success. One of AtD's stated goals is to create a culture of evidence. In the three schools presented in this chapter, some faculty took the charge very seriously.

Notes

1. AtD defines success as a grade of A, B, or C. For Pass/No Pass courses, success is defined as Pass.
2. DREAM is an annual conference conducted by AtD. Faculty and others in AtD colleges present sessions on "what works" in their colleges. Attendees can discuss their interventions and get tips for what they might do in their colleges.

References

Achieving the Dream. (2012). *Goal*. http://achievingthedream.org/
Adams, P., Gearhart, S., Miller, R., & Roberts, A. (2009). The Accelerated Learning Program: Throwing open the gates. *Journal of Basic Writing (CUNY)*, 28(2), 50–69.
Bell, R. K., Hill, D., & Lehming, R. F. (2007). *The changing research and publication environment in American research universities* (Working Paper SRS 07-204). Arlington,

VA: Division of Science Resources Statistics, National Science Foundation. Retrieved from http://www.nsf.gov/statistics/srs07204/

Bronfenbrenner, U. (1979). *Ecology of human development*. Cambridge, MA: Harvard University Press.

Bronfenbrenner, U. (1989). Ecological systems theory. In R. Vasta (Ed.), *Annals of child development: Vol. 6. Six theories of child development: Revised formulations and current issues* (pp. 187–250). Greenwich, CT: JAI Press.

Center for Community College Student Engagement. (2014). *Member colleges*. Retrieved from http://www.ccsse.org/aboutccsse/colleges.cfm

Cho, S. W., Kopko, E., Jenkins, D., & Jaggars, S. S. (2012). *New evidence of success for community college remedial English students: Tracking the outcomes of students in the Accelerated Learning Program (ALP)* (CCRC Working Paper No. 53). Retrieved from http://ccrc.tc.columbia.edu/media/k2/attachments/ccbc-alp-student-outcomes-follow-up.pdf

Cohen, A. M., & Brawer, F. B. (2003). *The American community college*. San Francisco, CA: Jossey-Bass.

Complete College America. (2012). *Time is the enemy*. Washington, DC: Complete College America. Retrieved from http://www.completecollege.org/docs/Time_Is_the_Enemy.pdf

Cross, K. P. (1990). Classroom research: Helping professors learn more about teaching and learning. In P. Seldin and Associates (Eds.), *How administrators can improve teaching: From talk to action in higher education* (pp. 122–142). San Francisco, CA: Jossey-Bass.

Hagedorn, L. S. (2010). The pursuit of student success: The directions and challenges facing community colleges. In J. C. Smart (Ed.), *Higher education: Handbook of theory and research* (Vol. 25, pp. 181–218). New York, NY: Agathon Press.

Hagedorn, L. S., Cabrera, A. F., & Prather, G. (2010). The community college transfer calculator: Identifying the course-taking patterns that predict transfer. *Journal of College Student Retention, 12*(1), 105–130.

Hoachlander, G., Sikora, A. C., & Horn, L. (2003). *Community college students: Goals, academic preparation, and outcomes* (NCES 2003–164). Washington, DC: National Center for Education Statistics, U.S. Department of Education.

Kuh, G. D., Jankowski, N., Ikenberry, S. O., & Kinzie, J. (2014). *Knowing what students know and can do: The current state of student learning outcomes assessment in U.S. colleges and universities*. Urbana, IL: National Institute for Learning Outcomes Assessment, University of Illinois and Indiana University. Retrieved from http://www.learningoutcomeassessment.org/knowingwhatstudentsknowandcando.html

Morest, V., & Jenkins, D. (2007). *Institutional research and the culture of evidence at community colleges*. Retrieved from http://files.eric.ed.gov/fulltext/ED499359.pdf

McClenney, K. M., & Arnsparger, A. (2012). *Students speak: Are we listening?* Lanham, MD: Rowman & Littlefield Publishers.

Nunley, C., Bers, T., & Manning, T. (2011). *Learning outcomes assessments in community colleges* (Occasional Paper #10). Urbana, IL: National Institute for Learning Outcomes Assessment, University of Illinois and Indiana University. Retrieved from http://www.learningoutcomeassessment.org/occasionalpaperten.htm

Rath, B., Rock, K., & Laferriere, A. (2013). *Pathways through college: Strategies for improving community college student success*. Hartford, CT: Our Piece of the Pie. Retrieved from http://www.opp.org/docs/PathwaysCollegeStrategies_StudentSuccess.pdf

Rutschow, E. Z., Richburg-Hayes, L., Brock, T., Orr, G., Cerna, O., Cullinan, D., ... Martin, K. (2011). *Turning the tide: Five years of Achieving the Dream in community colleges*. New York, NY: MDRC. Retrieved from http://www.mdrc.org/sites/default/files/full_593.pdf

Sandhills Community College. (2011). *Faculty job description and performance evaluation.* Retrieved from http://www.sandhills.edu/faculty-staff/syllabus/jobdescription .php

Selingo, J. (2000, November). Facing new missions and rivals, state colleges seek a makeover. *Chronicle of Higher Education, 47*(12), A40–42.

Sturgis, I. (2014, January 8). Gates Foundation invests half-billion in success of community college students. *Diverse Issues in Higher Education.* Retrieved from http://diverseeducation.com/article/59973/

Voluntary Framework for Accountability (VFA). (n.d.). Retrieved from http://vfa.aacc .nche.edu/Pages/default.aspx

White House. (2014). *Higher education.* Retrieved from http://www.whitehouse .gov/issues/education/higher-education

LINDA SERRA HAGEDORN is a professor of higher education in the School of Education at Iowa State University, and the associate dean of the College of Human Sciences at Iowa State University.

NEW DIRECTIONS FOR COMMUNITY COLLEGES • DOI: 10.1002/cc

6

This chapter describes the development of an applied research center at Atlantic Cape Community College and a statewide workforce training consortium run by the community college sector in New Jersey. Their contributions to the economic development mission of the colleges as well as their impact on the perception of community colleges by stakeholders are discussed.

Filling the Void: The Roles of a Local Applied Research Center and a Statewide Workforce Training Consortium

Richard C. Perniciaro, Lawrence A. Nespoli, Sivaraman Anbarasan

Many if not most community colleges include a commitment to economic development in their mission, vision, or goals statement. At Atlantic Cape Community College (2012), the strategic plan's vision statement contains the worthy goal that "Atlantic Cape Community College will be the region's preferred choice for higher education and professional training and a leading catalyst for economic and workforce development" (p. 4). In practice, most community colleges fulfill this part of their mission by training workers either through continuing education programs or through career-oriented associate in applied science degree programs—that is, they concentrate on the supply side of labor markets (McClure, 2010).

However, as the current economy has illustrated and Petrus (2014) has summarized, there is often a disconnect between the skills being taught by colleges and the needs of the local economy. Indeed, in areas like Southern New Jersey where unemployment and lack of employment growth have become the new normal, the opportunities for graduates are very limited on the local level where low-wage jobs are the only ones available as employees churn through the stagnant job market. In these conditions, students question the purpose of accumulating debt and forgoing current income to acquire skills for undefined careers. This leads to a lack of engagement by students and is a major cause of poor completion rates.

The Center for Regional and Business Research at Atlantic Cape Community College is one of a handful of contract-based economic/demographic research centers that uses the expertise of the staff of a community college to contribute to the demand side of the labor market equation. This chapter argues that efforts on this side of the equation provide mutual benefits to the community and the college on two fronts. On the one hand, the center provides valuable information to public and private sector decision makers in support of their efforts to spur local economic development activity. At the same time and precisely because of the role of the center in local economic development initiatives, important stakeholders in the community become more engaged, supportive, and influential in the future of the community college. These stakeholders include political leaders on the state and county levels responsible for funding the college, as well as the families who advise students on where to go to college and perhaps to consider the community college option as a way to keep the cost of attaining a 4-year degree affordable.

This chapter also describes how a statewide consortium of all New Jersey community colleges is similarly responding to the disconnect found between training programs and the needs of employers. By doing so, New Jersey's community colleges are successfully supporting both the supply side and demand side of New Jersey's labor markets in ways that are significantly enhancing the state's economic development efforts.

The Case for Applied Research at the Community College

In its assessment of the status of the community college in America at the turn of the millennium, *The American Community College Turns 100,* Educational Testing Service (2000) observed that the role of the sector to "provide a wide variety of services, responding to the needs of their communities and the businesses that operate within them, has also generated criticism about conflicts that arise from these multiple and sometimes conflicting roles" (p. 4). This is not a new criticism, but it raises the question of how to best reconcile these roles. Although most community college leaders would stress the primacy of the teaching role of their institutions, this sometimes leads to questions by external stakeholders about specific parts of the community college teaching mission. For example, in today's tough fiscal climate, political leaders and taxpayers are more likely to see community college remedial programs as expensive and duplicative of high school programs designed to prepare students for college.

As Goodvin et al. (2010) argue, the "perspective of these external stakeholders in regard to how they value the college's role in the community" leads to "the necessary modifications needed for the community college to move towards providing a higher level of service" (p. 3). These services must remain consistent with the needs of the stakeholders or their support will falter. And this chapter especially makes the case that these higher level services must include an expanded role for the community college in the economic development of the region. This role includes but is not limited to:

NEW DIRECTIONS FOR COMMUNITY COLLEGES • DOI: 10.1002/cc

- The ability to understand the needs of the local business community beyond the training of potential employees. The community college needs to assess and respond to the economic structure of the region in a proactive way, not just by providing a training service for the economy as it is or, too often, as it was in the past. This is a shift from skills training to a broader role in the economic development of the region.
- The ability to respond to the educational needs of the entire community including those students who will influence the economic structure of the region, not just those who will fit into the existing one. This means a larger role in science, technology, engineering, and mathematics (STEM) fields; entrepreneurship; and emerging industries in the region.

The services that need to be delivered to fulfill these roles are numerous and varied, and specific ones are described in a later section. However, the role of the Center for Regional and Business Research has provided a number of services related to regional development and the needs of the business community. In general terms, these have included the assessment of the strengths and weaknesses of the region or parts of the region in terms of growing existing businesses and nurturing new industries, assessing the role of workforce readiness in strengthening the region's economy, providing strategies for closing the gaps where weaknesses exist, and evaluating the actions taken by public agencies and private businesses to promote development and ensure that funds are spent in the most efficient means possible.

By providing these services, the college is able to engage with a whole new set of business leaders in the community while enhancing the general public perception of community colleges by potential students and members of their families. Too often the perception about community colleges for this group is guided largely by their own personal experiences as alumni of 4-year institutions.

These misperceptions about community colleges by business leaders and even by the general public lead to the wrong conclusion that the faculty and staff of community colleges have no interest in research or working with the business sector of the community. This can result in the loss of these community leaders as a potent political force for community colleges, which in most states rely in large part on local county taxpayer support for their funding.

Although low on the list of most community college promotion and tenure criteria, the need for faculty and staff to engage in applied research and provide a variety of business support services is a new imperative that many community colleges are struggling to meet.

As community college leaders attempt to reconcile the teaching and applied research roles of their institutions, it is important to understand the interrelationships between the two. This gives a different perspective and guidance for community college into the next decade and beyond.

These interrelationships were confronted head on by Ernest Boyer (1990) in his much referenced work *Scholarship Reconsidered*. In that work, he asks a critical question: "Is it possible to define the work of faculty in ways that reflect more realistically the full range of academic and civic mandates?" (p. 16).

His view of the functions of the professoriate points to the interrelationships between discovery, teaching, application, and integration as domains of scholarship. In this sense, it is not a separation but the connections among these four domains of scholarship that make the most sense. Although most community colleges recognize the discovery and teaching domains of scholarship, it is the scholarship of application and, even more, the scholarship of integration that holds the greatest potential for empowering community colleges to better serve the needs of their communities and important external stakeholders.

In Boyer's later work, he blended his treatment of application and integration research and in fact began to refer to the scholarship of application as the scholarship of engagement (Braxton & Luckey, 2010). Scholarship of application can be accomplished via the role of an observer. For example, service learning is a special case of the scholarship of application (Braxton, Luckey, & Helland, 2002). And indeed, many community college faculty have begun to engage in this kind of research by incorporating service learning components into career-oriented associate in applied science programs.

However, this is not the kind of research that will best support community college efforts to become active and engaged players in providing higher level services to business leaders. As Boyer suggests, it is only when research is connected to the faculty's field of knowledge and flows directly out of their professional activity that it rises to the level of the scholarship of engagement—the kind of scholarship this chapter sees as an important new service that community colleges and their faculty can offer to their local communities.

In short, the application of knowledge and, more than that, real engagement with the needs of the community are perfectly consistent with the primary teaching role long ago established by the community college sector. To avoid them is to miss an opportunity to change the perception of community colleges, which can be vital to capturing and retaining the attention of vital partners and stakeholders.

Creating an Applied Research Center

This chapter traces the origins and development of an applied research center at Atlantic Cape Community College designed to meet the specific needs of businesses in its local community. It goes without saying that other such centers at other colleges will similarly be responsive to their local communities while being mindful of competing services offered by other colleges or proprietary vendors.

NEW DIRECTIONS FOR COMMUNITY COLLEGES • DOI: 10.1002/cc

The resources to staff these centers may already be on campus, as many faculty members and administrators have performed applied research in the course of their studies or in prior or ongoing professional positions. In some cases, a cluster of fields can be assembled under one umbrella to provide a needed service. For example, the skills of institutional researchers, information technology staff, and marketing faculty can be combined in powerful ways to perform marketing research for interested business clients.

Assessing Community Needs.   There is a reason that there are very few community college applied research centers. In most instances, especially in large urban areas, there are other organizations that perform this function as a public interest. These can be educational institutions or regional economic development agencies with a vested interest in the health of the regional economy. However, in the case of southern New Jersey, these services by other organizations largely disappeared when the regional utility was consolidated with an out-of-state parent company.

Current web searches report active community college applied research centers at Kansas City Community College, Lorain County Community College in Ohio, and Cochise College in Arizona. These centers differ from the work of regional agencies in that they perform research on an as needed basis—a particular benefit to businesses that need information regarding their own activities. This more narrow function requires more than the ability to find, package, and report secondary data available through state and federal data centers. It requires one or more professionals on the staff that can generate primary research.

In the case of the Center for Regional and Business Research at Atlantic Cape Community College, a more proactive path was taken by the president whose position on the local workforce investment board (WIB) provided him direct access to economic and demographic research as a way to assess the labor needs in the college's local service area. Although the WIB had resources to train residents of the area, the skills that would be in demand in the future very often were misdiagnosed, leading to the inefficient use of resources and frustrated trainees.

Expanding the Role of the College and Its Faculty.   The lead author, as an executive of the regional electric utility at the time, was one of the mandated private sector representatives on the WIB. As a professional economist with experience in forecasting, modeling, market research, and economic development, the lead author provided staff support for many of the WIB committees through pro bono studies using the resources of the utility. At the time of the purchase of the utility by an out-of-state parent company, many of the corporate functions were consolidated at the home office, leaving the local area without professional resources at the disposal of community agencies.

Recognizing the needs of the community and the lack of committed research resources at other postsecondary institutions in the region, the president and lead author developed the structure of an applied research center at Atlantic Cape Community College to fulfill the needs of agencies such as the WIB. At the same time, the college was expanding its grants office to increase college revenues in response to the fiscal realities becoming apparent in the late 1990s. Having the internal capability to provide the analysis and information required by many grant applications would benefit the college's own fundraising efforts.

Organizationally, the Center for Regional and Business Research at Atlantic Cape Community College was created with certain stipulations. The center, run by the lead author, uses some college resources such as marketing, a small office, phone, computer, and office assistant services to conduct and promote its activities. However, the cost of these resources, in addition to the institutional salary of the lead author as director, is offset by grant and contract research for public and private sector clients, while providing a community presence at no cost. As there were no other applied research organizations in the region, the center did not compete with the private sector or other educational institutions for this business.

Finally, the center was able to use the expertise of faculty and staff at the college in proposals for competitive contracts and grants. In addition, the center uses services embedded in the college's core programs to offer a portfolio of services to clients. These have included, for example, the subcontracting of faculty members to do geographic information systems (GIS) mapping for a federal transportation grant and performing a marketing study for a potential culinary arts program at a community college in another state.

Institutional Structure. The center's administrative structure has evolved over time to meet the changing needs of external projects plus the internal needs of the college as well. First and foremost, the center director has been assigned additional college responsibilities including overseeing institutional research, assessment, and planning plus the college's capital construction projects.

The center's administrative functions are delivered by college staff, with the finance department helping with billing and other support staff maintaining an office presence for the center. In essence, the center has a virtual presence to the external community as its functions are distributed within the college to minimize expense. For example, with the professional oversight of the director, research needed for grants can be done through the college's institutional research office, and press releases are handled through the college's public relations department.

Research is also subcontracted to outsiders as necessary. When college employees are included in contract research, they receive payment as a stipend to their college pay.

The contributions of faculty members have been mostly concentrated in specialized areas such as GIS, social media, and health care—especially in competitive grants where their specific expertise is required. But because of their fixed teaching schedules and general lack of business experience, it is much more challenging for faculty to participate in the area of project management—assessing client needs, negotiating a scope of service, properly pricing the product, and directly dealing with the client. This is where the scholarship of engagement needs to be strengthened: by assisting faculty in developing the skills needed for consulting and project management. At the present time, colleges are not consistently compensating faculty members as they learn these skills. An institution wishing to grow a cadre of faculty and staff that can take part in engaging external stakeholders in roles beyond academic programs needs to dedicate resources to this endeavor. Unfortunately, most community colleges have not yet actively pursued this goal and budgeted resources to support it.

Regional Role of the Applied Research Center: Meeting Community Needs

As the Atlantic Cape Community College's Applied Research Center has matured over the past 15 years, its roles have evolved to meet the needs of the college's service area. In all of these roles, partnerships have been formed and the college has come to be seen as a source of high-quality and locally focused research. All of this has helped to enhance the credibility of the institution as a source of applied scholarship. In addition, these partnerships with organizations and agencies in the surrounding communities have also resulted in more resources being provided to the college to carry out its core workforce development and academic functions.

Grant Research.   The center has responded to the needs of both internal and external stakeholders seeking grants by providing analyses, coordinating the grant application process, and demonstrating need for funding based on regional economic conditions. At the same time, the center has actively supported related internal needs of the college. For example, the center provided data to demonstrate the impacts of Hurricane Sandy, which was the basis for a successful federal Trade Adjustment Assistance Community College and Career Training (TAACCCT) grant program.

In addition, the college routinely applies for state funding for business groups and consortia to receive workforce training grants through the New Jersey Department of Labor and Workforce Development. For example, the college's continuing education division is working with the local gas industry to establish a much-needed training program to help the unemployed qualify for jobs that sometimes go unfilled. These grants require economic research on the local labor market, and the resulting programs have been an ongoing source of relationship building with corporate sectors, especially gaming, in the region.

Another key external stakeholder groups in the region is the healthcare sector. When this sector was faced with a serious nursing shortage in the early 2000s, the college was quick to respond with a needed expansion of its registered nursing (RN) program. However, because of the nursing shortage, the college was itself having trouble finding qualified faculty members who could supervise students in clinical settings. Working through the WIB, the college partnered with area providers including hospitals and visiting nurse services to seek grant funding from the Robert Wood Johnson Foundation to fund a study to find solutions to these expansion issues. The center wrote portions of the needs assessment section of the grant application, and the nursing faculty defined the programmatic changes needed for expansion. Once funded, the center acted as the official grant evaluator under contract to the WIB.

This began a much wider partnership with the healthcare industry, including shared funding for qualified clinical supervisors who became a part of the nursing program plus a new paramedic program using new modes of instruction to make the program shorter and available to those already engaged in the healthcare profession.

Public Service.   Another key role of the center is providing public service to the community. This comes in many forms, each of which provides a relationship to local external stakeholder groups as well as to other community leaders who sit on boards and advisory committees. This public service occurs in several ways.

Information Clearinghouse.   The center director is recognized as a key source for much-needed regional economic data and information. Local chambers of commerce and governmental planning offices typically do not have their own research staff to gather this information, so they regularly look to the center director to provide it for them.

In addition, the center is regarded by regional news outlets as an unbiased source of opinion and analysis. Often featured and quoted in local and statewide news outlets, the center is widely seen as a valuable resource for the region. And because of its affiliation with Atlantic Cape Community College, there is value added to the public perception of community colleges throughout the state.

Informal Consultation.   When asked to do so, the center has offered consulting advice on an informal basis to elected officials at the local, county, and state levels. The center director often testifies about the economic conditions and possibilities for the region at local planning hearings and state legislative committees. These sessions often include discussion of the educational and training needs of local residents, a primary function of the college.

Contract Research Projects.   The center has established itself as a source of high-quality research, as evidenced by the award of competitively solicited contracts to it, as well as by the number of repeat clients who have had positive experiences with past research done by the center. In fact, the center has developed a number of niche markets, deploying faculty members where their specific skill sets serve a project well.

School District Enrollments.   As in most states, New Jersey school districts need to compete for state funds for capital improvements. In addition, capital bonds are sometimes paid for by local taxpayers. With the state department of education, school district administrators, and taxpayers as stakeholders in this funding process, the center is able to demonstrate value to the community by participating in this funding process.

Serving as the demographer of record, the center provides enrollment projections to numerous school districts, both large and small, throughout the region. Local schools appreciate this service provided by the center, and it adds value to the overall work the college does with the K–12 sector throughout its service area.

Economic Impact Studies.   Another niche market for the center is economic impact studies. These have been a source of revenue as well as a source of good publicity for the college. These studies are frequently requested as part of a grant application (required for certain federal grants such as those administered by the Federal Highway Administration and the Economic Development Administration), by a business wanting to demonstrate its contribution to the local economy, or by an agency or advocacy group to demonstrate their impact to their stakeholders. The center typically uses a model and methodology developed by the U.S. Bureau of Economic Analysis for consistency and legitimacy.

Clients have included public agencies as well as private businesses—from a private glass company seeking zoning approval to expand, to the Greater Atlantic City Chamber of Commerce Annual Air Show, to a number of Ladies Professional Golf Association tournaments throughout the country, to the impact of a Coast Guard training facility on the local economy.

Market Research Studies.   If there is one service that especially requires an intimate knowledge of the local economy and thus the need for an applied research center at the local level, it is market research studies. For instance, although Cape May County in New Jersey has a high unemployment rate and the wages are below state averages, the market is driven by second-home owners, who tend to be fairly wealthy—a fact that cannot be found in census information.

Recognized as a research entity with local knowledge, the Applied Research Center at Atlantic Cape Community College has had clients as diverse as a specialty grocery store interested in locating in the area, to a municipal government seeking a better way to market its recreational and business assets to potential visitors.

Economic/Demographic Projections.   The center has successfully received contracts in open bidding projects from the regional South Jersey Transportation Planning Organization and the South Jersey Economic Development District, both federal agencies. In both cases, projections for a multicounty area have been used to prioritize the distribution of federal funds. These projects have involved meetings with focus groups made up of political leaders as well as county and local planners. The results—long-term forecasts at the municipal level—are used by local governments for grants and funding resources.

NEW DIRECTIONS FOR COMMUNITY COLLEGES • DOI: 10.1002/cc

Economic Development Strategies.   The center also prepares economic development strategies for cities, towns, and the region. These are done using the methodology required by the U.S. Economic Development Administration's Comprehensive Economic Development Strategy (CEDS) program. This allows the client to use the study, if desired, to apply for funding from this agency. These projects require meetings with all stakeholders in the area under consideration as well as open public meetings. The exposure for the center and college is extensive and has led to very positive long-term relationships.

The center has performed these studies both under subcontract to other vendors and independently. These have spanned six states. Working with the South Jersey Economic Development District on its CEDS led to the birth of an aviation studies program at the college, which has resulted in increased partnerships between the Federal Aviation Administration Technical Center, the aviation research community, and the college. Additionally, this research was later used to develop successful grants, which resulted in the college receiving an air traffic control simulator worth nearly $300,000 plus another million dollars for its recently completed STEM building.

In summary, the presence of an applied research center, in areas of expertise that have a demonstrated community need, provides the college with partnerships that are closely connected to existing or future academic areas; revenues that help to offset the costs of the center; and, as explained next, a new value-added proposition for external stakeholders whose decisions have an impact on the shape and purpose of the college.

Changing the Perception of the Community College Through Applied Scholarship

The evolution of the Applied Research Center at Atlantic Cape Community College must be considered in the context of the geography, economy, and existing fiscal climate in which the college finds itself. The processes the center uses in responding to community needs are much the same regardless of the specific client and the particulars of the client's needs. However, the key to any of these efforts is the ability of the college to demonstrate added value to external stakeholders from a resource base that exists at all community colleges—an educated and specialized faculty. The payoff for these efforts falls into the three main categories.

Value of Partnerships.   This is a value proposition from which both sides can benefit. Meeting partners on their own terms and in response to their own needs gives them ownership of the mission of the college.

Reaching External Stakeholders.   The center has been an important vehicle through which the college has been able to reach political and potential donor stakeholders, who greatly value the services that the center provides. However, to further enhance the perception of the community college as a place with high-quality programs and staff, the applied research capabilities of the institution must somehow be shared with parents and potential students too. This can serve as an additional rebuttal to the perception that community colleges are not a place for those interested in research or collaboration with the private sector.

This group of stakeholders can be reached more easily once credibility in the quality of the programs offered can be demonstrated externally. The college needs to be seen as a place where prepared students can get more than just the first few courses needed to transfer to a 4-year college.

Changing the Internal Culture.   The internal culture of higher education institutions values and rewards the development of professional knowledge, but often does not offer similar rewards for sharing that knowledge with community and political leaders. This is the most fundamental argument for expanding the role of faculty in the kinds of services offered by college-based applied research centers. A too frequent complaint by many clients about working with college faculty is that the faculty do not fully understand client needs. This can change only through more collaborations between faculty and clients in applied research projects.

New Jersey Community College Consortium: A Statewide Collaboration to Provide Workforce Training Solutions

The lessons learned at Atlantic Cape Community College's Applied Research Center are evident as well in a statewide consortium created by New Jersey's community college presidents in 2004. Through the consortium, the colleges have joined together to develop and deliver new customized training programs, which have reached many new external stakeholder groups while at the same time enhancing the perception of community colleges throughout the state.

The original idea behind the consortium was a simple one. The goal was to say to businesses, "If you have a training need, we can help by delivering the *combined* expertise and resources of New Jersey's community colleges to your employees, no matter where your business is located."

Since then, the consortium's popular training programs have grown consistently. Over the past 10 years, more than 120,000 employees at over 5,000 businesses have received training.

The power of this statewide collaboration has recently been brought to bear on a new training model that relies heavily on applied research. Appropriate college faculty are recruited to work with the consortium staff to conduct industry and job data research. Based on this research, faculty then design curricula that are delivered across the state and lead to national credentials.

Called "Training on Demand," this new training model addresses two of the state's biggest labor market challenges: (a) a scarcity of trained entry-level workers in many industries and (b) a scarcity of jobs for the unemployed. It does this by matching businesses in need of skilled workers with job seekers who have been trained and certified in the skill sets demanded by those businesses, often through statewide organizations such as New Jersey Business and Industry Association.

Here's how the program works. First, the consortium identifies companies in a particular industry that are seeking skilled workers with comparable skill sets. Next, the consortium trains and certifies job seekers for that same industry who have passed screening tests for motivation and aptitude.

The participating companies also have a role to play. They help design the training, interview prospective trainees, and commit to hiring program graduates. The training is typically underwritten with state and federal grants so that it can be provided free of charge to participating businesses and unemployed workers. Recent examples include metal fabrication, computerized numerical control (CNC) machining, and production technology leading to national industry credentials along with college transfer credits.

The success of this Training on Demand model is perhaps best captured in a comment by a high-level official in the New Jersey Department of Labor and Workforce Development, which has helped fund the program since its inception. Although the department has for years spent a lot of money on training grants, too often, he noted, "it kept its fingers crossed that the training would lead to good jobs." Now, by working with the Community College Consortium, the state is achieving much more successful job placement rates.

By participating in this process and by conducting industry research in collaboration with employers, faculty help to create curricula for various career pathways, which in turn are accepted into related certificate associate degree programs. Such curricula are becoming increasingly popular at many New Jersey community colleges institutions because they lead to competency-based credit certificates and associate degrees when combined with other traditional requirements for college education.

Closing Observation

Whether at the local or state level, community college faculty are uniquely positioned to be highly qualified resources on a wide variety of issues and thus can play a key role in providing the kinds of higher level services offered to businesses and other community organizations through campus-based applied research centers. Faculty also have an especially integral role in identifying job demand patterns through research in key industries and developing curricula along career pathways.

It is time to firmly establish this applied research presence as one of the key roles of community colleges nationally. At a time when our colleges (and the government agencies that fund them) are facing unprecedented fiscal pressures, the value of community college programs and services in their local communities and throughout the states must be strengthened and expanded with new ideas and new relationships. In short, the time to encourage and promote applied scholarship at community colleges is now. There is no question that the kinds of applied research discussed in this chapter can increasingly be done by community college faculty.

References

Atlantic Cape Community College. (2012). *Strategic plan 2012–2016.* Mays Landing, NJ: ACCC.

Boyer, E. L. (1990). *Scholarship reconsidered: Priorities of the professoriate.* San Francisco, CA: Jossey-Bass.

Braxton, J. M., & Luckey, W. (2010). Ernest Boyer and the scholarship of engagement. In H. E. Fitzgerald, C. Burack, & S. Seifer (Eds.), *Handbook of engaged scholarship: Contemporary landscapes, future directions* (pp. 71–92). Lansing: Michigan State University Press.

Braxton, J. M., Luckey, W., & Helland, P. (2002). *Institutionalizing a broader view of scholarship through Boyer's four domains* (ASHE-ERIC Higher Education Report, Volume 29, Number 2). San Francisco, CA: Jossey-Bass. Retrieved from http://files.eric.ed.gov/fulltext/ED468779.pdf

Educational Testing Service. (2000). *The American community college turns 100: A look at its students, programs, and prospects.* Princeton, NJ: ETS. Retrieved from http://www.ets.org/Media/Research/pdf/PICCC.pdf

Goodvin, S., Bakken, L., Eubank, H., Rathman, S., Watkins, M., Stucky, J., ... Jaradat, M. (2010). *Neosho County Community College: A study of external stakeholders' perspectives.* Wichita, KS: Wichita State University. Retrieved from https://web.neosho.edu/ICS/icsfs/WSU_NCCC_Final_Report_4_28_10.pdf?target=df953ec6-7e6c-44c5-9b81-14f030e64eec

McClure, A. (2010, March). Community colleges as economic saviors. *University Business.* Retrieved from http://www.universitybusiness.com/article/community-colleges-economic-saviors

Petrus, M. H. (2014). *Workforce development challenges in Ohio.* Cleveland, OH: The Federal Reserve Bank of Cleveland. Retrieved from https://www.clevelandfed.org/en/Newsroom%20and%20Events/Publications/Special%20Reports/sr%2020140210%20workforce%20development%20challenges%20in%20ohio.aspx

RICHARD C. PERNICIARO, PHD, *is the director of the Center for Regional and Business Research at Atlantic Cape Community College and the vice president of planning, research, facilities and executive support.*

LAWRENCE A. NESPOLI *is the president of the New Jersey Council of County Colleges, the state association for New Jersey's community colleges.*

SIVARAMAN ANBARASAN *is the executive director of the New Jersey Community College Consortium for Workforce and Economic Development.*

7

This chapter contends that scholarship should become a part of the mission of the community college. The authors describe actions for individual community colleges and state and federal actions that encourage and support the engagement of community college faculty members in scholarship.

Tweaking the Culture of the Community College

John M. Braxton, William R. Doyle, Dawn Lyken-Segosebe

The teaching mission of the community college and teaching as the primary role of faculty members in community colleges must remain ascendant. We posit, however, that scholarship should become a part of the mission of the community college. In particular, the mission of community colleges should embrace the scholarships of application, integration, and teaching.

We offer this bold recommendation for three reasons. First, community college faculty members already show a pattern of engagement in these three domains of scholarship either in the form of publications or in the form of unpublished, but publicly observable, outcomes of scholarship (Braxton & Lyken-Segosebe, Chapter 1). Such outcomes constitute scholarship given Shulman and Hutchings's (1998) assertion that an unpublished outcome of scholarship may be designated as scholarship if it meets three necessary characteristics: (a) it must be publicly observable, (b) it must be amenable to critical appraisal, and (c) it must be in a form that permits its exchange and use by other members of a scholarly community. More specifically, more than two fifths of community college faculty members have published one to two times within the scholarship of integration domain within the past 3 years, the majority of community college faculty members report they have produced one to two times unpublished outcomes of scholarship associated with the domains of application and of integration, and more than half of community college faculty members report that they have produced three to five times forms of unpublished outcomes of scholarship associated with the scholarship of teaching during the past 3 years (Braxton & Lyken-Segosebe, Chapter 1). In

NEW DIRECTIONS FOR COMMUNITY COLLEGES, no. 171, Fall 2015 © 2015 Wiley Periodicals, Inc.
Published online in Wiley Online Library (wileyonlinelibrary.com) • DOI: 10.1002/cc.20156

77

addition, scholars of pedagogical practice exist as a distinct type of faculty scholars in community colleges (Park, Braxton, & Lyken-Segosebe, Chapter 2). The work of scholars of pedagogical practice aligns with the scholarship of teaching as a domain. Such engagement in scholarship by community college faculty members currently occurs within an "organizational culture that at best views scholarship as a personal and optional endeavor that faculty members can pursue if they wish and at worst as an abrogation of the institution's student-focused values" (Palmer, Chapter 4, p. 38).

The second reason stems from the need for scholarship by community college faculty members focused both on teaching and on service to the community. Townsend and Twombly (2007) state that providing access to higher education stands as a societally allocated mission for the community college. To fulfill this mission, community colleges must maintain an open door admissions policy that sets aside such selection criteria as previous academic performance and academic tests (Townsend & Twombly, 2007). As a consequence, community college faculty members teach a wide range of students. Teaching such a wide range of students creates a need for scholarship focused on the development and refinement of pedagogical practice (Morest, Chapter 3), a goal of the scholarship of teaching (Braxton, Luckey, & Helland, 2002). Likewise, scholarship that serves the local community is also needed. Service to the community has historically been identified as part of the mission of the community college (Dougherty & Townsend, 2006). In Chapter 6, Perniciaro, Nespoli, and Anbarasan delineate ways in which one community college serves its local community through the scholarship of application. These ways include conducting enrollment projections of student enrollment to school districts in the region served by the college, conducting economic impact studies, and conducting market research. These ways clearly resonate with goals of the scholarship of application as the use of disciplinary knowledge and skills to address important societal and institutional problems (Boyer, 1990).

The diffident professional identity of community college faculty constitutes the final reason. A professional identity remains elusive for community college faculty. Despite early recognition in the works of Garrison (1967), Cohen (1973), and Cohen and Brawer (1972, 1977, 1996, 2008), the gap between employment as teachers and membership in an identified profession remains within the community college professoriate (Palmer, 1992). That a professional identity remains elusive for community college faculty finds evidence in Cohen and Brawer's (2008) more recent version of *The American Community College* in which they state that "the disciplinary affiliation among community college faculty is too weak, the institutions' demands of scholarship are practically nonexistent, and the teaching loads are too heavy for that form of professionalism to occur" (p. 107). Scholars (Cohen & Brawer, 2003; Eaton, 1994; Levin, Kater, & Wagoner, 2006; Outcalt, 2002; Palmer, 1992; Prager, 2003; Vaughan, 1988) propose that involvement in scholarship, especially the scholarship of teaching, affords an opportunity to strengthen the professional identity of the community college.

These reasons indicate a need for the tweaking of the culture of community colleges to regard scholarship by faculty members as worthy of some degree of institutional support and encouragement rather than viewing "scholarship as a personal and optional endeavor that faculty members can pursue if they wish and at worst as an abrogation of the institution's student-focused values," as Palmer says in Chapter 4 (p. 38). As a consequence, we describe in this chapter some actions that individual community colleges and governmental policy makers might take to tweak the culture of the community college to provide some support for the engagement of their faculty in scholarship. However, the engagement in scholarship by community college faculty must not become the "assumptive world of the academic professional" (O'Meara, 2011, p. 191) as exists in 4-year colleges and universities.

Actions for Individual Community Colleges

We offer seven actions that individual community colleges might take to support and encourage engagement in scholarship by their faculty members. These approaches pertain to full-time faculty in the community college. These actions do not privilege community college faculty members holding doctoral degrees over those faculty who do not, given Braxton and Lyken-Segosebe's finding in Chapter 1 that faculty holding doctoral degrees differ little from their colleagues who do not hold a doctoral degree in their levels of engagement in the four domains of scholarship. Each of these actions sustains the practice of regarding scholarship as personal and optional faculty activity but provide full institutional support and encouragement for those faculty electing to engage in scholarship. We describe each of these actions next.

1. The mission of the college should include some statements about scholarship focused on application, integration, and teaching being goals of the institution. Such statements should also include a discussion of the value of these forms of scholarship to the students served by the college (the scholarship of teaching), the lay public (the scholarships of application and integration), or the local community (the scholarship of application).

2. A second action entails establishing an expectation for engagement in scholarship for promotion to full professor. However, effective teaching should remain the primary criterion for promotion to full professor. Thus, the criteria for promotion to full professor would include publications or unpublished, but publicly observable, outcomes of scholarship reflective of the scholarships of application, integration, and teaching or types of faculty scholars such as immersed scholars, scholars of dissemination, scholars of pedagogical

practice, and localized scholars (Park, Braxton & Lyken-Segosebe, Chapter 2). Unpublished, but publicly observable, outcomes of scholarship include such outcomes as papers presented at meetings of professional associations, audio- or videotaped presentations, reports, videos, computer software, and websites (Braxton & Del Favero, 2002). Such outcomes meet the three criteria posited by Shulman and Hutchings (1998) for an unpublished outcome of scholarship to be designated as scholarship: (a) it must be publicly observable, (b) it must be amenable to critical appraisal, and (c) it must be in a form that permits its exchange and use by other members of a scholarly community. Although we favor making scholarship an expectation for promotion to full professor, we do not recommend that it become an expectation for tenure. Making scholarship an expectation for tenure could result in the displacement of effective teaching as the preeminent mission and goal of the community college.

3. Individual community colleges should consider the creation of the professorial title of Professor of the College. Faculty awarded this title should exhibit a record of both effective classroom teaching and of engagement in scholarship reflective of the scholarship of application, integration, or teaching or as immersed scholars, scholars of dissemination, scholars of pedagogical practice, or localized scholars (Park, Braxton, & Lyken-Segosebe, Chapter 2).

4. Individual community colleges should permit full-time faculty to enter into creativity contracts. Boyer (1990) describes creativity contracts as a vehicle for establishing flexible and varied career paths for professors. He notes that faculty experience periods of ebbs and flows in their careers (Boyer, 1990). Faculty members should be given the freedom to alter the focus of their work and delineate professional goals for 3- to 5-year periods of time (Boyer, 1990; Braxton et al., 2002). The full-time community college faculty who has devoted his or her career to teaching may welcome an opportunity to dedicate more time to engagement in scholarship through a reduction in the teaching load. The professional goals delineated might include a focus on the development and refinement of pedagogical practice or application of disciplinary knowledge and skills to the local community.

5. Individual community college should provide funds for faculty to attend academic and professional meetings especially if presenting a paper. Both Morest (Chapter 3) and Palmer (Chapter 4) allude to the role of professional associations in fostering the scholarship of community college faculty members. In particular, Palmer describes the efforts of various disciplinary associations to acknowledge the work of the community college. In Chapter 4, Palmer lists the American Mathematical Association of Two-Year Colleges, the Two-Year College English Association, and the Committee on Physics in Two-Year Colleges of the American Association of Physics Teachers as examples of such

professional disciplinary associations. Community colleges should provide some travel support for faculty to attend the meetings of such associations.

6. Teaching occupies 85% of the typical community college faculty member's time (Rosser & Townsend, 2006). For community college faculty to devote more time to teaching, community colleges must provide some ways to alter their teaching loads. Possible actions include temporary reductions in teaching course load, mini-sabbaticals, release time during the academic year, and summer salary support (Braxton et al., 2002). Community college might offer these ways for alterations in teaching loads to faculty planning to submit their materials for promotion to full professor or to faculty who have entered into creativity contract agreements.

7. Community colleges should establish centers for research in service of the local community. Such a center would serve as a clearinghouse for matching local organizations requiring disciplinary knowledge and skill to address their needs with community college faculty members with the requisite knowledge and expertise to conduct the needed research. Put differently, such a center would provide opportunities for community college faculty to engage in the scholarship of application. The Center for Regional and Business Research at Atlantic Cape Community College described by Perniciaro, Nespoli, and Anbarasan in Chapter 6 offers a good model for such a center.

These actions that individual community colleges can take to foster the engagement in scholarship by community college faculty do not function within a vacuum as state and federal policies can work to bolster these institutional actions. In the next section, we describe such state and federal actions policy makers may take.

State and Federal Actions

Community colleges are closely tied to federal and state policy in ways that even their public 4-year counterparts may not be. Community colleges are highly dependent on state appropriations for unrestricted revenue, and a high proportion of students in community colleges depend on state and federal grant aid (Baum, Little, & Payea, 2011; Palmer, 1996). Because community colleges are entities that are closely tied to state and federal policy, it is crucial that policy makers be involved in discussions of scholarship for community college faculty.

State and federal policy in the area of community college faculty scholarship should focus on ways to motivate both faculty and institutions to engage in public scholarship. It would be much less appropriate and possibly counterproductive to attempt to regulate scholarship among community college faculty. All of the following recommendations are premised on the idea of fostering further scholarship through the creation of incentives. In addition, all of these changes are intended to be relatively low cost. Community colleges are already underfunded relative to 4-year institutions, and substantial additional funds should not be diverted from either hiring full-time faculty or supporting students for the purpose of increasing scholarship (Levin & Kater, 2012). As the ideas outlined here demonstrate, it may be possible to gain a substantial increase in scholarship for a relatively small investment.

Performance Funding.   Many states now have some form of outcome-based funding, and more states are considering adopting such a funding strategy. These funding programs shift the emphasis in state support for higher education from funding on the basis of enrollment to funding on the basis of preferred outcomes. For instance, in Tennessee, community colleges are funded on the number of students who accumulate certain numbers of credit hours, transfers, graduates, and so on (Dougherty & Reddy, 2013). In addition to these outcome-based funding formulas, many states also include small amounts (less than 5% of overall funding) in the form of performance funds (Burke, 2002). These performance funds would be an ideal place for state policy makers to encourage additional scholarship from community college faculty.

A performance funding initiative that supported additional scholarship from faculty at community colleges could support the second action from the previous section—requiring visible scholarship for promotion to full professor at community colleges. States could provide a funding bonus of 0.5% to 1% of overall funding based on the number of visible forms of scholarship produced by faculty at a community college, with agreed-upon definitions based on the framework described by Shulman and Hutchings (1998). Institutions that put in place requirements for visible scholarship for promotion would be much more likely to attain these performance goals and receive this additional funding. This would create a much-needed incentive for administrators to change promotion guidelines.

Incentive Funds.   States could also create small incentive funds for individual faculty members at community colleges to pursue visible forms of scholarship. These incentive funds would typically include small grants or additional salary for community college faculty who complete visible works of scholarship, including the usual types of scholarship such as published books or articles, and alternative forms of visible scholarship as described previously. The primary requirement would be that the scholarship be visible and relevant to the community college mission. It is important that such funding remain an extra incentive and not be built into base salaries for community college faculty as a whole, as funding such a broad-based change in salary is unlikely to be feasible for many states.

Union Contracts.   In many states, community faculty jointly bargain for salary, benefits, and working conditions. In these states, such arrangements form a key basis for policymaking for community college faculty (Gerber, 2014). States with collective bargaining agreements should seek to incorporate the actions described previously, particularly the requirement that faculty engage in visible scholarship. Such agreements should carefully specify the acceptable formats for scholarship and the expectations for promotion to senior faculty positions.

Seed Funding for Local Partnerships.   States that wish to support the scholarship of application among community college faculty in service to their community should consider creating seed funding for faculty and administrators. Such funding could be combined with funding from localities, school districts, and local businesses to create innovative research centers at community colleges focused on local needs. One design that states could consider would be to offer "matching funds" for community colleges that seek research funding from other sources, including the business community. Successful applicants for such seed funding would be required to be faculty at community colleges who would produce visible scholarship in service of relevant local goals. Such centers should be intended in the long run to be self-sustaining but could be given much needed start-up assistance through state "venture capital" funds.

Federal Initiatives.   At the federal level, policy makers should consider structuring federal grant programs so that faculty at community colleges can engage in scholarship. The Department of Education through the Institute of Education Sciences (IES) has already begun funding research partnerships that involve a collaboration between practitioners and faculty or researchers (U.S. Department of Education, 2014). In the area of community colleges, IES could reward additional engagement in such partnerships by community college faculty collaborating with faculty at research institutions.

The Obama administration has proposed a joint federal–state funding program that promises free tuition at community colleges for the first 2 years for many students. One of the conditions of receipt of these funds is that community colleges use evidence-based methods for improving student success (White House Office of the Press Secretary, 2015). Although this is a laudable goal, the evidence supporting interventions to improve community college success is notably thin (Calcagno, Bailey, Jenkins, Kienzl, & Leinbach, 2008). Many community college faculty members have been closely involved in the design, implementation, and evaluation of such interventions but do not have many incentives for publishing the results of these evaluations in traditional formats. The federal government should consider engaging community college faculty in research on effective interventions to produce student success, with an emphasis on the creation of visible forms of scholarship based on effective interventions.

Closing Thoughts

All of these recommendations seek to ensure that faculty at community colleges who wish to engage in further scholarship have available to them a set of resources that make it feasible to do so. In addition, administrators at community colleges should have sufficient incentives to ensure that their faculties are supported in this endeavor. By recognizing that community college faculty have been engaged in scholarship and could form the basis of promising centers of scholarship in the future, these efforts could improve community colleges, their local areas, and the lives of students. Moreover, these recommendations work toward tweaking the culture of the community college to provide some support for the engagement of their faculty in scholarship while not dislodging teaching as the preeminent mission of the community college.

References

Baum, S., Little, K., & Payea, K. (2011). *Trends in community college educa-tion: Enrollment, prices, student aid, and debt levels.* New York, NY: The College Board. Retrieved from https://trends.collegeboard.org/sites/default/files/trends-2011-community-colleges-ed-enrollment-debt-brief.pdf

Boyer, E. L. (1990). *Scholarship reconsidered: Priorities of the professoriate.* Princeton, NJ: The Carnegie Foundation for the Advancement of Teaching.

Braxton, J. M., & Del Favero, M. (2002). Evaluating scholarship performance: Tradi-tional and emergent assessment templates. In C. L. Colbeck (Ed.), *New Directions for Institutional Research: No. 114. Evaluating faculty performance* (pp. 19–32). San Fran-cisco, CA: Jossey-Bass.

Braxton, J. M., Luckey, W., & Helland, P. (2002). *Institutionalizing a broader view of schol-arship through Boyer's four domains* (ASHE-ERIC Higher Education Report, Volume 29, Number 2). San Francisco, CA: Jossey-Bass.

Burke, J. C. (2002). *Funding public colleges and universities for performance.* Albany, NY: SUNY Press.

Calcagno, J. C., Bailey, T., Jenkins, D., Kienzl, G., & Leinbach, T. (2008). Community college student success: What institutional characteristics make a difference? *Eco-nomics of Education Review, 27*(6), 632–645.

Cohen, A. M. (Ed.). (1973). *Toward a professional faculty.* San Francisco, CA: Jossey-Bass.

Cohen, A. M., & Brawer, F. B. (1972). *Confronting identity: The community college in-structor.* Englewood Cliffs, NJ: Prentice-Hall.

Cohen, A. M., & Brawer, F. B. (1977). *The two-year college instructor today.* New York, NY: Praeger Publishers.

Cohen, A. M., & Brawer, F. B. (1996). *The American community college* (2nd ed.). San Francisco, CA: Jossey-Bass.

Cohen, A. M., & Brawer, F. B. (2003). *The American community college* (4th ed.). San Francisco, CA: Jossey-Bass.

Cohen, A. M., & Brawer, F. B. (2008). *The American community college* (5th ed.). San Francisco, CA: Jossey-Bass.

Dougherty, K. J., & Reddy, V. (2013). *Performance funding for higher education: What are the mechanisms? What are the impacts?* (ASHE-ERIC Higher Education Report, Volume 39, Number 2). San Francisco, CA: John Wiley & Sons.

Dougherty, K. J., & Townsend, B. K. (2006). Community college missions: A theoretical and historical perspective. In B. K. Townsend & K. J. Dougherty (Eds.), *New Directions for Community Colleges: No. 136. Community college missions in the 21st century* (pp. 5–13). San Francisco, CA: Jossey-Bass.

Eaton, J. S. (1994). *Strengthening collegiate education in community colleges.* San Fran-cisco, CA: Jossey-Bass.

Garrison, R. H. (1967). *Junior college faculty: Issues and problems—A preliminary national appraisal.* Washington, DC: American Association of Community and Junior Colleges.

Gerber, L. G. (2014). *The rise and decline of faculty governance: Professionalization and the modern American university.* Baltimore, MD: Johns Hopkins University Press.

Levin, J. S., & Kater, S. T. (2012). *Understanding community colleges.* New York, NY: Routledge.

Levin, J. S., Kater, S., & Wagoner, R. (2006). *Community college faculty: At work in the new economy.* New York, NY: Palgrave Macmillan.

O'Meara, K. (2011). Faculty civic engagement: New training, assumptions, and markets needed for the engaged American scholar. In J. Saltmarsh & M. Hartley (Eds.), *To serve a larger purpose: Engagement for democracy and the transformation of higher education* (pp. 177–198). Philadelphia, PA: Temple University Press.

Outcalt, C. (2002). *A profile of the community college professorate, 1975–2000.* New York, NY: RoutledgeFalmer.

Palmer, J. (1992). Faculty professionalism reconsidered. In K. Kroll (Ed.), *New Directions for Community Colleges: No. 79. Maintaining faculty excellence* (pp. 29–38). San Francisco, CA: Jossey-Bass.

Palmer, J. C. (1996). *Funding the multipurpose community college in an era of consolidation.* Paper submitted to the American Education Finance Association. Retrieved from http://eric.ed.gov/?id=ED396783

Prager, C. (2003). Scholarship matters. *Community College Journal of Research and Practice, 27,* 579–592. doi:10.1080/10668920390194499

Rosser, V. J., & Townsend, B. K. (2006). Determining public 2-year college faculty's intent to leave: An empirical model. *The Journal of Higher Education, 77*(1), 124–147.

Shulman, L. S., & Hutchings, P. (1998). *About the scholarship of teaching and learning: The Pew scholars national fellowship program.* Menlo Park, CA: The Carnegie Foundation for the Advancement of Teaching.

Townsend, B. K., & Twombly, S. B. (2007). *Community college faculty: Overlooked and undervalued* (ASHE-ERIC Higher Education Report, Volume 32, Number 6). San Francisco, CA: Jossey-Bass.

U.S. Department of Education. (2014). *Researcher–practitioner partnerships in education research.* Retrieved from http://ies.ed.gov/funding/ncer_rfas/partnerships.asp

Vaughan, G. B. (1988). Scholarship in community colleges: The path to respect. *The Educational Record, 69*(2), 26–31.

White House Office of the Press Secretary. (2015). *Fact sheet—White House unveils America's College Promise proposal: Tuition-free community college for responsible students.* Retrieved from https://www.whitehouse.gov/the-press-office/2015/01/09/fact-sheet -white-house-unveils-america-s-college-promise-proposal-tuitio

JOHN M. BRAXTON *is a professor of education in the Higher Education Leadership and Policy Program at Peabody College of Vanderbilt University.*

WILLIAM R. DOYLE *is an associate professor of higher education and public policy in the Higher Education Leadership and Policy Program at Peabody College of Vanderbilt University.*

DAWN LYKEN-SEGOSEBE *received her PhD in leadership and policy studies from Vanderbilt University.*

Appendix: Description of Research Methods and Analyses for Chapters 1 and 2

John M. Braxton

This appendix describes the methodology and statistical procedures used to obtain the findings presented in the following two chapters: Chapter 1, "Community College Faculty Engagement in Boyer's Domains of Scholarship," and Chapter 2, "Types of Faculty Scholars in Community Colleges." This appendix also contains the tables referenced in these two chapters.

Methodology: Sample and Data Collection for Chapters 1 and 2

Full-time faculty members holding tenured, tenure-track, and non-tenure-track academic appointments at community colleges in four academic disciplines—biology, chemistry, history, and sociology—constitute the population of inference for this study. A sample of 200 community colleges—suburban and urban of all categories—was randomly selected from this population; all faculty members from each of the four academic disciplines were selected from the sampled community colleges. A total of 2,352 faculty members were selected using this cluster sampling design. The Faculty Professional Performance Survey was e-mailed as an online survey using Survey Monkey to this sample of faculty members in spring 2012. This survey included professional behaviors reflecting each of the four domains of scholarship. Two experts on faculty scholarship performance provided face validity for these professional behaviors. These behaviors were developed using the work of Boyer (1990), Braxton and Toombs (1982), and Pellino, Blackburn, and Boberg (1984) as a foundation. This survey also contained items measuring characteristics of the faculty such as full- or part-time status, race/ethnicity, academic rank, highest degree completed,

New Directions for Community Colleges, no. 171, Fall 2015 © 2015 Wiley Periodicals, Inc.
Published online in Wiley Online Library (wileyonlinelibrary.com) • DOI: 10.1002/cc.20157

and tenure status. Braxton, Luckey, and Helland (2002) developed The Faculty Professional Performance Survey for their research on faculty engagement in each of Boyer's four domains of scholarship in 4-year colleges and universities. We modified this survey for use with community college faculty members. This research was approved for execution by the Institutional Review Board for the Protection of Human Subjects of Vanderbilt University.

After an initial e-mail and four additional e-mails to nonrespondents, a total of 485 faculty members completed the online survey instrument. However, 28 e-mails were designated as "bounced" and 17 respondents opted out. This reduced the initial base sample size of 2,352 to 2,307. This sample size provided the basis for the calculation of the response rate of 21%. The final sample size of 485 was further reduced to 348 by restricting our subsequent analyses to full-time faculty members only. We conducted t-tests and chi-square analyses comparing initial respondents to the survey with individuals who responded to subsequent e-mails on the seven dependent and three independent variables of this study. This method of ascertaining sample bias is consistent with the formulation of Goode and Hatt (1952) and Leslie (1972). These tests indicated that the sample of 348 full-time community college faculty members tends to be representative of the population of inference on six of the seven dependent variables and on two of the three independent variables. More specifically, the obtained sample demonstrated a slight bias toward faculty with higher levels of unpublished outcomes of scholarship: teaching domain as faculty who responded to the initial e-mail evidenced higher levels of such productivity than did faculty members who responded to subsequent e-mails. In addition, faculty members with a disciplinary association with chemistry tend to be underrepresented in the sample of 348 full-time community college faculty members. Thus, a sample comprising 348 full-time community college faculty members was used in Chapter 1.

For Chapter 2, Park, Braxton, and Lyken-Segosebe formed an analytic sample of 188 faculty members who held tenured or tenure-track positions from the sample of 348 faculty members described previously. This sample is more restrictive than that of Braxton and Lyken-Segosebe (Chapter 1) who used full-time faculty but did not confine the sample to tenured or tenure-track faculty members. Results from t-tests and chi-square analyses comparing initial respondents to the survey with individuals who responded to follow-up e-mail reminders to nonrespondents indicate that respondents tend to be representative of the population.

Variables

For Chapter 1, our research design consists of seven dependent and three independent variables. The seven dependent variables fall into two categories. One category consists of publications reporting the outcomes of in the four domains of scholarship from their colleagues who do not have a doctoral degree? We used independent t-tests to address this research question with highest earned degree as the independent variable for each of the seven t-tests we conducted, a t-test for each of the seven dependent variables. We performed these seven tests at the .05 level of statistical significance. We show the results of these t-tests in a table available from the first author of Chapter 1.

Statistical Analysis for Research Question Three: Do community college faculty members' levels of engagement in the four domains of scholarship vary by their academic rank? In addressing the third question, we conducted one-factor analyses of variance. Academic rank functioned as the factor composed of four levels: professor, associate professor, assistant professor, and instructor. We executed seven analyses of variance, one for each of the seven dependent variables. We performed these analyses of variance at the .025 level of statistical significance. We used this more conservative level of statistical significance to reduce the probability of committing type I errors because we detected heterogeneous variances prior to conducting these analyses of variance. We exhibit the results of these analyses of variance in a table available upon request to the first author of Chapter 1.

Statistical Analysis for Research Question Four: Do community college faculty members' levels of engagement in the four domains of scholarship vary across different academic disciplines? We attended to this question by executing seven one-factor analyses of variance, one for each of the seven dependent variables. Academic discipline served as the factor composed of four levels: biology, chemistry, history, and sociology. We carried out these analyses of variance at the .025 level of statistical significance to reduce the probability of committing type I errors given that we identified heterogeneous variances prior to conducting these analyses. Table A.2 shows the results of these analyses of variance.

Statistical Procedures for Chapter 2

Park, Braxton, and Lyken-Segosebe used cluster analysis to identify ways in which faculty scholarship behaviors at community college group together. Put differently, they used a statistical approach that attempts to group faculty members based on their scholarly activity. They used Ward's method of clustering (Ward, 1963) to empirically discern these groups of faculty based on their scholarship. The Ward method attempts to minimize the variance within each cluster—in other words, the method seeks to form clusters whose members are tightly related to one another based on their engagement in scholarship. Following the cluster analyses, Park, Braxton, and Lyken-Segosebe first computed descriptive statistics for the clusters and then undertook a discriminant analysis to assist in naming the clusters as is common in the process of cluster analysis (Huberty & Lowman, 1998).

Table A.2.   Analyses of Variance of Community College Faculty Engagement in the Four Domains of Scholarship by Academic Discipline (Full-Time Faculty)

Domain/Form of Engagement	F-Ratio	Means by Academic Discipline				Post Hoc Mean Comparison
		Biology	Chemistry	History	Sociology	
Publications oriented toward the Scholarship of Application	3.390*	1.0372	1.0509	1.0656	1.200	Sociology and History greater than Biology*
Unpublished outcomes of Scholarship: Application Domain	4.268**	1.2880	1.2009	1.4194	1.3622	History greater than Chemistry*
Publications oriented toward the Scholarship of Discovery	4.484**	1.0443	1.0250	1.1129	1.1750	No statistically significant differences
Publications oriented toward the Scholarship of Integration	5.037**	1.0627	1.0176	1.1327	1.2014	Sociology greater than Chemistry**
Unpublished outcomes of Scholarship: Integration Domain	11.432**	1.1496	1.1036	1.3625	1.3487	History and Sociology greater than Biology and Chemistry**
Publications oriented toward the Scholarship of Teaching	3.130	1.0417	1.0221	1.0805	1.1571	No statistically significant differences
Unpublished outcomes of Scholarship: Teaching Domain	2.346	2.5252	2.4172	2.5833	2.7949	No statistically significant differences

*$p < .025$.
**$p < .01$.

Cluster Analysis Results

Three clusters emerged from the data analysis, and Table A.3 presents the characteristics of the faculty respondents in the analytic sample as well as across the three clusters. A table that presents raw score means for the survey items by cluster is available from the first author upon request.

NEW DIRECTIONS FOR COMMUNITY COLLEGES • DOI: 10.1002/cc

INDEX

AACC. *See* American Association of Community Colleges (AACC)

AAPT. *See* American Association of Physics Teachers (AAPT)

ABA. *See* American Bar Association (ABA)

Accelerated Learning Program (ALP), 58–59

ACCT. *See* Association of Community College Trustees (ACCT)

Achieving the Dream: Community Colleges Count (AtD), 49

Achieving the Dream colleges, faculty research in, 49–60; Achieving the Dream project, 51–52; background of, 50–51; at Community College of Baltimore County, 57–59; development spheres of faculty, 59; faculty research, definition of, 52–53; at Macomb Community College, 55–57; overview, 49; at Temple College, 54–55

Adams, P., 59

Advanced Technological Education (ATE) program, 29–30

ALP. *See* Accelerated Learning Program (ALP)

AMATYC. *See* American Mathematical Association of Two-Year Colleges (AMATYC)

AMATYC News, 40

American Association of Community Colleges (AACC), 31

American Association of Physics Teachers (AAPT), 38

American Bar Association (ABA), 28

American Community College Turns 100, The, 64

American Mathematical Association of Two-Year Colleges (AMATYC), 28, 38–42

American Sociologist, The, 46

Anbarasan, S., 3, 63, 75

Andelora, J., 39, 41–46

APA Committee of Psychology Teachers at Community Colleges (PT@CC), 28

Applied research, 63–75; at community colleges, 63–75; at Atlantic Cape Community College, 66–72; benefits to community college, 72–73; case for, 64–66; at New Jersey Community College Consortium, 73–74

Applied research center, at Atlantic Cape Community College: assessing community needs, 67; college and faculty role, 67–68; creation of, 66–69; grant research, role in, 69–70; institutional structure and, 68–69; public service, role in, 70–72; regional role of, 69–72

Arnsparger, A., 50

Association of Community College Trustees (ACCT), 51

ATE program. *See* Advanced Technological Education (ATE) program

Austin, A., 1, 9, 11

Bailey, T., 24, 83

Bakken, L., 64

BATEC. *See* Boston Area Advanced Technological Education Connections (BATEC)

Bauerlein, M., 42

Baum, S., 81

Bell, R. K., 52

Bers, T., 50

Bio-Link, 30

Blackburn, R. T., 87

Blair, R., 42

Boberg, A. L., 87

Boston Area Advanced Technological Education Connections (BATEC), 30

Boyer, E. L., 2, 7–9, 12, 15, 21–23, 30–32, 66, 78, 80, 87

Brawer, F. B., 1, 24, 38, 50, 78

Braxton, J. M., 2, 4, 5, 7–9, 13–15, 17–19, 23, 31, 32, 66, 77, 78, 80, 81, 85, 87–89, 91, 93, 95

Brock, T., 52

Bronfenbrenner, U., 59, 60

Bucher, R., 37, 44

Burke, J. C., 82

Cabrera, A. F., 50
Calcagno, J. C., 83
Carnegie Academy for the Scholarship of Teaching and Learning (CASTL), 30
Cascadia Community College (CCC), 33
CASTL. *See* Carnegie Academy for the Scholarship of Teaching and Learning (CASTL)
CCBC. *See* Community College of Baltimore County (CCBC)
CCC. *See* Cascadia Community College (CCC)
CCFSSE. *See* Community College Faculty Survey of Student Engagement (CCFSSE)
CCSSE. *See* Community College Survey of Student Engagement (CCSSE)
Center for Community College Student Engagement, 51
Cerna, O., 52
Chickering, A. W., 33
Cho, S. W., 58
Ciccone, A., 30
Cody, C. C., 46
Cohen, A. M., 1, 24, 38, 50, 78
Cohen, D., 42
Committee on Physics in Two-Year Colleges (CPTYC), 38, 40–42
Community College Faculty: Overlooked and Undervalued, 13, 23
Community college faculty research, in AtD colleges, 49–60; Achieving the Dream project, 51–52; background of, 50–51; at Community College of Baltimore County, 57–59; definition of, 52–53; at Macomb Community College, 55–57; overview, 49; at Temple College, 54–55
Community College Faculty Survey of Student Engagement (CCFSSE), 25
Community College of Baltimore County (CCBC), 57–59
Community College Survey of Student Engagement (CCSSE), 51
Community Dimension of the Community College, The, 18
CPTYC. *See* Committee on Physics in Two-Year Colleges (CPTYC)
Creswell, J. W., 9
Crocker-Lakness, J., 1

Cross, K. P., 53, 55, 56, 60
Cullinan, D., 52

Del Favero, M., 13, 23, 32, 80
Dougherty, K. J., 78, 82
Doyle, D. A., 46
Doyle, W. R., 4, 77, 85

Eaton, J. S., 1, 78
Enger, J., 41, 42
Eubank, H., 64
Everyday Math, 56

Faculty engagement, in Boyer's domains of scholarship, 7–14; implications for practice, 12–13; overview, 7–9; research methods and analyses of, 87–95; findings on, 9–11
Faculty scholars, empirically derived, 15–19; immersed scholars, 16; overview, 15–16; recommendation for, 17–18; research methods and analyses of, 87–95; scholars of dissemination, 16–17; scholars of pedagogical practice, 17
Faculty scholarship, and community college culture, 21–35; ATE program, 29–30; background of, 22–24; examples of, 29–32; expansion of, 32–33; external influences on, 27–29; faculty work and, 24–25; internal influence on, 26–27; overview, 21–22; recommendations for, 34–35; service learning and, 31–32
Feldman, K. A., 15

Gad-el-Hak, M., 42
Gamson, Z. F., 33
Garrison, R. H., 78
GCC. *See* Guttman Community College (GCC)
Gearhart, S., 59
Gerber, L. G., 82
Ginder, S. A., 21
Glassick, C. E., 15
Goode, W., 88
Goodvin, S., 64
Grody, W., 42
Grubb, W. N., 23, 26, 27
Guidelines for Two-Year College Physics Programs, 42
Guttman Community College (GCC), 33

Hagedorn, L. S., 3, 49, 50, 62
Hargens, L., 9
Harlacher, E., 18
Hatt, P., 88
Hein, W., 40
Helland, P., 8, 9, 13, 15, 23, 31, 66, 78, 80, 81, 88, 89
Hill, D., 52
Hoachlander, G., 50
Honored But Invisible, 23
Horn, L., 50
Huber, M. T., 15, 30
Huberty, C. J., 91
Hutchings, P., 8, 13, 15, 77, 80, 82

Ikenberry, S. O., 50
Institutionalizing a Broader View of Scholarship Through Boyer's Four Domains, 9

Jaggars, S. S., 58
Jankowski, N., 50
Jaradat, M., 64
Jeandron, C., 31
Jenkins, D., 24, 53, 58, 83
Journal of Basic Writing, 59

Kater, S., 1, 26, 27, 43, 44, 78, 82
Kelly-Reid, J. E., 21
Kienzl, G., 83
Kinzie, J., 50
Kisker, C. B., 38
Knapp, L. G., 21
Kopko, E., 58
Kroll, K., 44
Kuh, G. D., 50

Laferriere, A., 50
Lehming, R. F., 52
Leinbach, T., 24, 83
Leslie, L. L., 88
Levin, J. S., 1, 26, 27, 43, 44, 78, 82
Little, K., 81
Lowman, L. L., 91
Luckey, W., 8, 9, 13, 15, 23, 31, 66, 78, 80, 81, 88, 89
Lyken-Segosebe, D., 2, 4, 7, 14, 15, 19, 77, 85, 88, 91, 93

Macomb Community College, 55–57
Maeroff, G. I., 15
Manning, T., 50

Martin, K., 52
MathAMATYC Educator, 40
McClenney, K. M., 50
McClure, A., 63
McKelvey, B., 42
Melguizo, T., 24
Middaugh, M. F., 22, 23, 32
Miller, R., 59
Monroe, M. B., 40–42
Morest, V. S., 2, 21, 36, 53
Mullin, C. M., 27
Murray, J. P., 23, 26

NAEYC. See National Association for the Education of Young Children (NAEYC)
National Association for the Education of Young Children (NAEYC), 28
National Institute for Staff and Organizational Development (NISOD), 55
National Survey of Postsecondary Faculty-2004 (NSOPF:04), 7, 23
Nespoli, L. A., 3, 63, 75
New Jersey Community College Consortium, 73–74
NISOD. See National Institute for Staff and Organizational Development (NISOD)
Nunley, C., 50

O'Kuma, T. L., 40–42
O'Meara, K., 79
Orr, G., 52
Outcalt, C. L., 1, 78

Palmer, J. C., 1, 3, 12, 13, 37, 38, 43, 48, 78, 81
Park, T. J., 2, 15, 17–19, 88, 91, 93
Paulsen, M. B., 15
Payea, K., 81
Pellino, G. R., 87
Perniciaro, R. C., 3, 63, 75
Petrus, M. H., 63
Poulsen, S. J., 33
Prager, C., 1, 78
Prather, G., 50
Professional identity of community college faculty, 37–47; barriers and facilitators to scholarship, 42–44; faculty advocacy for scholarship, 44–47; overview, 37–39; professional organizations and, 39–42

Rath, B., 50
Rathman, S., 64
Reddy, V., 82
Research and Scholarship in the Two-Year College, 44
Rice, E., 8
Richburg-Hayes, L., 52
Roberts, A., 59
Robinson, G., 31
Rock, K., 50
Rogers, E. M., 29
Rosser, V. J., 1, 7, 23, 81
Rutschow, E. Z., 52

SATA. *See* Scientific and Advanced Technology Act (SATA)
SCATE. *See* South Carolina Advanced Technological Education Center–Center of Excellence (SCATE)
Scholarship in community colleges, actions for: by community colleges, 79–81; federal initiatives, 83; incentive funds, 82; overview, 77–79; performance funding, 82; seed funding for local partnerships, 83; by state and federal governments, 81–83; union contracts, 82–83
Scholarship of teaching and learning (SOTL) activities, 30–31
Scholarship Reconsidered: Priorities of the Professoriate, 7, 66
Scientific and Advanced Technology Act (SATA), 29
Segosebe, D. L., 19
Seidman, E., 1
Selingo, J., 52
Service learning, and faculty scholarship, 31–32
Shulman, L. S., 8, 13, 15, 77, 80, 82
Sikora, A. C., 50
SOTL activities. *See* Scholarship of teaching and learning (SOTL) activities

South Carolina Advanced Technological Education Center–Center of Excellence (SCATE), 30
Spalter-Roth, R., 46
Stelling, J. G., 37, 44
Stucky, J., 64
Sturgis, I., 52

TCCTA. *See* Texas Community College Teachers Association (TCCTA)
Teaching and Learning Academy (TLA), 31
Teaching English in the Two-Year College, 40
Temple College, 54–55
Texas Community College Teachers Association (TCCTA), 55
TLA. *See* Teaching and Learning Academy (TLA)
Toombs, W., 87
Townsend, B. K., 1, 7, 13, 23, 24, 26, 38, 78, 81
Trade Adjustment Assistance Community College and Career Training (TAACCCT) grant program, 69
Trimble, S. W., 42
Twombly, S. B., 13, 23, 24, 26, 38, 78
Two-Year College English Association (TYCA), 38–42
TYCA. *See* Two-Year College English Association (TYCA)

Vaughan, G. B., 1, 40, 45, 46, 78
VFA. *See* Voluntary Framework for Accountability (VFA)
Vitullo, M. W., 46
Voluntary Framework for Accountability (VFA), 51

Wagoner, R. L., 1, 26, 27, 43, 44, 78
Ward, J., 91
Watkins, M., 64
Wulff, D., 1, 9, 11